M000306979

"Mental toughness is spartanism with qualities of sacrifice, self-denial, dedication. It is fearlessness, and it is love."

—**Vince Lombardi**

No Punches Pulled.

Also by Scott Allan

Empower Your Thoughts

Empower Your Deep Focus

Rejection Reset

Rejection Free

Relaunch Your Life

Drive Your Destiny

The Discipline of Masters

Do the Hard Things First

Undefeated

Fail Big

Nothing Scares Me

No Punches Pulled

Bust Through Mental Boundaries, Develop a Resilient Mindset, and Forge Bulletproof Self Discipline

by Scott Allan

Copyright © 2021 by **Scott Allan Publishing** all rights reserved.

No Punches Pulled: Bust Through Mental Boundaries, Develop a Resilient Mindset, and Forge Bulletproof Self Discipline by Scott Allan

All rights reserved. No part of this book may be reproduced in any form without permission in writing from the author. Reviewers may quote brief passages in reviews.

While all attempts have been made to verify the information provided in this publication, neither the author nor the publisher assumes any responsibility for errors, omissions, or contrary interpretation of the subject matter herein.

The views expressed in this publication are those of the author alone and should not be taken as expert instruction or commands. The reader is responsible for his or her own actions, as well as his or her own interpretation of the material found within this publication.

Adherence to all applicable laws and regulations, including international, federal, state and local governing professional licensing, business practices, advertising, and all other aspects of doing business in the US, Canada or any other jurisdiction is the sole responsibility of the reader and consumer.

Neither the author nor the publisher assumes any responsibility or liability whatsoever on behalf of the consumer or reader of this material. Any perceived slight of any individual or organization is purely unintentional.

ISBN (Paperback): 978-1-990484-11-7

eISBN (eBook): 978-1-990484-09-4

ISBN (Hardcover): 978-1-990484-10-0

Download this <u>Free Training</u>:
Bulletproof Stealth Habits

CONTENTS

"Your toughness is made up of equal parts persistence and experience. You don't so much outrun your opponents as outlast and outsmart them, and the toughest opponent of all is the one inside your head."

—Joe Henderson

Introduction

The match was down to 2–2. I needed one more point to win, and my opponent—poised and ready to strike—stared me down from the other side of the mat. Everything was riding on my ability to move fast and get in under his sidekick that was certain to come. How did I know this? I had studied this opponent for a long time, watched him beat most of the guys on my team, and now, somehow, I had made it to the final round and was ready to claim the prize.

It was Osaka, 2012, and I had entered my seventh karate tournament for that year. Although this wasn't my first tournament, it was the first match where I'd made it to the finals.

This was it. I was the Karate Kid, Bruce Lee, and Chuck Norris all wrapped into one. I had trained hard to get here, put in the hours at the dojo, and now, with thousands watching from the sidelines, it all came down to these last few moments. I was wearing the white flag and my opponent was wearing the red.

In karate tournaments, when a point is scored, the spotters outside the ring raise the flag when points are scored.

2–2. Next point wins. I had never felt so alive. Adrenaline was coursing through my body, my mind a dopamine mess ready to come unraveled.

As we braced for the final round, the judge placed a hand between us in the center of the ring. With a final "Hai!" the fight started.

And this is when it happened. I could sense a shift in my confidence, like when you're riding the rollercoaster and, on the long drop down, your heart leaps into your throat as the coaster defies gravity, carrying you toward the bottom of the funnel before surging upward again.

Downward spiral at fifty miles an hour. It was like that, and as my mind dropped its guard, my opponent sensed the hesitation, like a dog can smell fear. He moved in, and I retreated. In previous matches, I counterattacked or stayed fixed on an opening.

This was different. I had this feeling that I was going to lose, as if I had given up already and just wanted it over. Screams from the side urged me to move in, to do one of my "moves" that had gotten me to this stage. But like that deer when it freezes in headlights, my body failed to respond.

I dodged a kick, but as my mind moved into survival mode, I could sense myself backing away to the edge of the mat. Helpless, hopeless, without anywhere to maneuver, and unable to "think," it was like watching a film in slow motion. Where I was certain I had this fight, a momentary lapse of mental weakness—accelerated by the thought of "I'm going to lose"—is all it took.

But this was not where I failed. My opponent was confident, and his overconfidence left a momentary opening that I immediately lasered in on. I pushed the fear out of my mind and stepped around his kick, moving in with a right punch that had won many points in the past. And just before my right fist should have connected with his midsection, that feeling of doubt and hesitation hit me again. And when it did, I failed on the follow-through. I mean, one moment I had it, and the next second, I pulled the punch at the last microsecond.

And the chance was gone.

The one move I had been trained to watch for—his sidekick—came straight on center mass, lifted me up and off my feet, and everything came crashing in. The force of the kick didn't hurt, but the momentary shock of knowing I was finished definitely sank in as I sank to the mat, more as a sign of defeat than anything.

And *that* was *that*.

I walked away with a second-place trophy, but it wasn't what I wanted. It's not just that I wanted to win. Everybody wants to win. But the fact that I knew I could have won because I had what it takes. I had trained and worked for it. My hesitation in that moment caused fear and fear led to panic. Panic became desperation.

Desperation becomes uncertainty. It was my moment of uncertainty that cost me the match.

I walked away that day with a second-place trophy, and a lesson in life that would change everything.

Hesitation Leads to Lost Opportunity and Failure

No Punches Pulled comes from the concept that, if you fail to follow through with your "punch," you will fail to win the match. Your opponent—competition, adversary, or enemy—will sense this sudden weakness and strike first. You inevitably lose the match, and in life, these same rules apply.

To hesitate in life—to pull your punches—means that fear got the best of you. When the mind responds to fear-based thoughts, it signals to the brain and body that danger is near, and you enter into flight mode. I lost the tournament match because I failed to follow through. But it wasn't until after the defeat that I began to recognize a lifelong pattern in my failure to follow through.

I always hesitated before making a decision, and in most cases, leaving things to the last minute until I had to do something. In relationships, I would rarely, if ever, initiate conversation. At parties, I hesitated to speak up first. My mind was always there, warning of the potential dangers I faced with rejection or vulnerability. Just as I had pulled back in the tournament, I could now see how this one pattern of self-sabotage had hijacked my freedom to be me, to push forward, and to win.

Like most people, I wanted to win in life. But wanting to and making a clear decision you definitely will are balanced on a fine line. When fear wins, you jump into the shallow end of the pool because it's safer. I could see hesitation in many forms in my day-to-day interactions. I would rarely speak up, and even then, it was when prompted to "just say something!"

When you hesitate to take intentional action, you settle for second best. Or third. You lose your dreams because only people who follow through with what they say they are going to do really make it.

But the one thing I was living with that injured me the most was regret. I continued to revisit the moments of the tournament. Then I would go back further in time and regret not seizing the opportunities I had been given. The people I never met or the jobs I could never have as that part of me—the self-doubting, broken part—continued to play the same story in my mind. That story sounded like this:

"You're not good enough. Don't do it. You don't deserve it. Who do you think you are? What are you doing here? Can't you see that everyone is better than you are? Don't you know that you're expected to lose because you always have?"

I could hear the voice in my head as I became fully aware of its presence. It was then that a moment of clarity happened. I could hear the voice and see its self-loathing. It was the voice of all doubts and fears. It was the voice of failings and regrets. It was a voice from the past that I had been listening to on autopilot. It controlled my hesitation and injected a reality of fear into my life that I had always believed to be "normal." You never question your own mind when it shows up as your best friend every day. This was not a friend but an alter ego I had to defeat.

I knew if I defeated this cloud of doubt, I would never pull my punches again. I would have no fear or anxiety walking into a crowded room or engaging in a discussion where people exchanged ideas. I would value myself as someone who matters. I would do all the things that I was afraid of doing because I no longer feared the outcome of losing or looking foolish.

In a moment of regret, I had found a way out, a solution to all my problems. I decided to act differently, think differently, and engage differently. This one decision cleared the way for a new frame of mind to be built. The voice I listened to demanded attention, but instead, I fed my mind with new thoughts. I now had an obsession with becoming the best, but not to defeat someone in a karate match.

It was to defeat my own mind, take control of it, and rebuild the foundations that had weakened. If there is a dark side in all of us, this had become my mission: to venture down the road less traveled and discover for the first time who I was. More importantly, the potential of everything I could be.

This "No Punches Pulled" principle can be applied to many things in our life. If you don't follow through with a job interview, you'll never get the job you want. If you don't approach someone to ask for help, you'll never learn the right approach. If you fear taking action for fear of failing, you will never know what you are capable of achieving.

Following through with my punches in karate was just as important as following through with everything else in life. By committing to the "punch" (decision, action, commitment), you are willing to accept the outcome even if you end up losing.

Just as my punches failed to land most of the time, sometimes they connected. Similarly, most jobs you apply for, you will never get. Most risks you take, you will likely fail. Most companies that start a business, end up going out of business within five years.

The odds are good that most punches you throw will fail to connect. But not leaning hard into your punch will cause you to miss 100%.

Turning Doubt into a No Punches Pulled Action Plan

Doubt is a term that describes a lack of trust in oneself. The truth is, many people doubt themselves when they must take intentional action and move against the obstacles that are holding them back. Their self-doubt isn't the barrier people think it is; it's a necessary step that they must work through before they achieve success.

You don't have to wait for confidence to show up before you do something that scares you. You don't need courage before you act. You gain confidence after you overcome your moments of self-doubt. Confidence is like motivation; if we wait for it show up, we could spend a lifetime waiting.

The confidence comes when you act; if the first step is self-doubt in any situation, the next step builds your confidence. You feel better about what you can really do when you do what needs to be done first.

If you experience doubt when you're facing a new challenge, that's good. It's a sign that you're stepping out of your comfort zone. You're worried that you could fail.

You risk losing something, and by challenging that doubt, you push it out of the way.

Believing in your doubts and giving up empowers your sense of failure; you leverage your power when you move against it.

Self-doubt is always temporary. As soon as you get out there and do it, it's diminished. It might show up again the next day, but that's because you're pushing the envelope again, going further, breaking out of the fear-based zone. Think about anything you tried the first time and you'll remember that you were loaded with self-doubt.

Can I do this?

Should I do this?

What if I don't do this?

What if I fail my first time?

The loop comes back to the fear of failing. It's the old antagonist of every success story. The fear of failure is a lack of faith in yourself to succeed. If you buy into its power, you'll always have it.

People who are afraid to leap, fear the unknown. You'll hear the voices of people warning you against it: They may say, "You'd better not jump. Nobody has ever made it this far."

They may say, "That's risky. I know so many people who have died trying." Yes—and I know many who died without trying but wished on their deathbed that they had tried.

They may say, "You don't know what's out there."
That's true. But if I just sit here in the same place, doing
what I've always done, I'll *never* know what's out there.

You never know what's out there until you go looking for it.

A Brief Story

When I finished college twenty years ago, I made a
daring choice. The economy at the time was depressed,
and there weren't many jobs in my field. A friend of
mine who lived out west in Vancouver suggested I move
there because the place was booming, and everyone had
work.

Now, I come from a small town, and I'll be honest; I had
never traveled or moved very far from home. In fact, I
was pretty set on staying where I was. I had a girlfriend,
and we were madly in love. I was going to marry her, live
in a small house, and have kids and a couple of dogs.

I spent most of my days drinking in the local pub and
enjoying the life. I didn't have a lot of ambition other
than getting a job and staying in my hometown.

But my friend's offer was on my mind. Then, he sent me
pics of the city. My initial fear of leaving home turned
into a deep interest.

This changed into a powerful drive to do something
more with my life than just sit around, watching life pass
me by. The more I thought about it, the more excited I
started to feel, but there were lots of voices in my head at
play. They sounded like this:

·   *"What if you get out there and you hate it? You'll have to come
home a failure."*

· *"What about your girlfriend, and the house and two dogs you talked about?"*

The voices wanted me to stay. They wanted an easy life. They wanted to believe the fear. But I knew that wasn't an option.

I told my parents about my idea. They knew I wanted to do more with my life. I knew that too. There was a force inside me that wouldn't rest. You can call it "the call to destiny" or whatever you like, but if you've ever taken a chance on something that scared the hell out of you because you knew you had to do it, then you know what this is.

I decided to do it. I had a gut full of fear every day. I set the departure date. Three months from now. I was going to do it. I realized in my moment of decision what courage really is: taking a leap of faith without confidence, embracing your doubt, and jumping in anyway.

As Forrest Gump said, *"My momma told me, 'Life was like a box of chocolates. You never know what you're gonna get.'"*

There are no guarantees in this life. If you're waiting for a guarantee before you take that leap, you'll be waiting until the end of your life. Seize your doubt and jump in if you feel it's right.

The next day, my father showed up with an itinerary and a plane ticket. He handed it to me and said: "This is your ticket to a new life. Now go make it."

I hadn't asked for the ticket. It was a gift. Three months later, full of doubt and uncertainty, I boarded a plane to an unknown destination with no guarantees, and $500 in my pocket. I had a carry-on with a pair of jeans and socks. What it came down to was this: I had two types of fear.

One was the fear of going and not knowing what I was getting into, afraid that things wouldn't work out or I would get homesick.

The other was the fear of staying in a small town and never seeing the world, never knowing what's out there, and never knowing how far I could possibly go. It was the fear of not being an explorer but just sitting around in a bar on a barstool all day talking about all the things I was going to do "someday."

I wonder at times where I'd be if fear #2 had not been stronger than fear #1. Again, it wasn't about making the right choice, but stepping out of the zone, embracing that fear and taking a chance on something that I really wanted.

When you have no choice, it's the only choice.

I made it to the other side and never looked back. My fear center had expanded, and I was doing things I had never dreamed possible. Years later, I moved to Japan and explored the depths of Asia. I traveled and had adventures. What had been a fear of not knowing what was out there became a passion for discovery.

Why am I telling you this story? Because there are two sides to the journey. Two people, actually. You're living a double life. There's the person you are, and the person you could be. Maybe self-doubt is holding you back. You're worried about something bad happening.

Well, remember that years from now, we will look back on our lives and ask, "Did I do everything I could have done to make the best life possible? Did my fear stop me from living a bold and daring adventure?"

The lesson to learn: There are no negative outcomes. Guarantees are for cars and home appliances. There are no guarantees you'll make it if you leap, but if you don't take the chance or the risk, you'll be guaranteed to stay where you are.

I lived in a "stuck zone" for many years. Fear of the unknown made sure I stayed there. Facing your uncertainty and saying, "Well, here goes," guarantees your success—regardless of what happens.

People get stuck when they doubt their chances of success. They weigh all the options, the good and the bad, and ask others for advice about what to do. Something that a mentor once told me is this:

"Fear is always with you. It isn't about becoming fearless and then taking action. You become fearless by taking action, or at the very least, you fear everything much less after you take the initiative."

I look at confidence-building like this: It's a massive puzzle that takes a long time to build; you just have to keep putting the pieces together. You have to start *somewhere* with *something*. It doesn't matter if it's a mini goal of cleaning out an old closet.

Confidence is the other side of living in fear. People who exist in a permanent state of fear are holding themselves back from doing. They think that they're going to lose out somehow. They doubt all ability to succeed.

You can build your confidence up by getting busy. An earlier mentor of mine once said, "You're held back by the mind that's between your own ears. Nobody is taking over your mind except you. Own it and you're free."

Kill your doubt before it kills your dreams. If there's something you're dying to do with your life, and you're being held back, remember that you're not going to live forever. Make the most of the day. It's a better alternative than regretting the things you never did.

In this book, I'm going to teach you a system of lessons that can change your life, and provide you with a winning system for crushing existential self-doubt, building a bulletproof mind and pushing you out of your comfort zone.

Let's get started. We have a lot to learn.

"It takes energy, mental toughness and spiritual reinforcement to successfully deal with life's opportunities, and to reach your objectives."

—Zig Ziglar

Build Laser-Focused Clarity
(and do whatever it takes)

"Clarity precedes success."

Robin Sharma

All around you, there are likely to be stated different concepts and laws for success and happiness. Some will say you can't have it all. Others will make grand promises that you *can* have it all. But the truth is, most people will never figure out exactly what it is that they want in the first place. Or they will, but only once it is too late.

A television host once asked H. L. Hunt, a man with a classic rags-to-riches story of going from farming in cotton plantations to becoming an oil magnate, what his biggest piece of advice was for those chasing success. Hunt reportedly said, "One needed just two things—to know exactly what one wants, and the price he's willing to pay to get it."

This advice is so critical that you must imprint this into your mind:

- Know what you want.
- Decide what price you're willing to do to get it.

That's where most people fail. They get this very first step on the ladder to success wrong. You must be clear about what you want, and only then, can you figure out a path to get there.

We live in a day and age where we're constantly inundated with information, both relevant and irrelevant. We're on top of exactly what our peers are doing, including details such as where they last vacationed and when they got a big promotion. It's a world of constant comparisons, confusion, and a fear of being left out, fueled by perfectly curated Instagram feeds and snarky Tweets.

It's very easy to get lost. It's easy to get overwhelmed. It's easy to get frustrated. It's easy to forget what you stand for and lose sight of the values that make you the most *you*. In this land of confusion, it is—quite simply—very easy to fail, and not understand why.

When you don't have this steady *inner compass* to guide you, you're viewing the world in terms of reactions to triggers rather than in terms of perspectives and decisions aligned with your core set of values. In such a case, by default, you will always find yourself where you don't belong pursuing things you don't need and ending up with something you don't want.

When life is not going your way, it's because you aren't making decisions aligned with your values and your life vision. Perhaps you want what others have because it looks so irresistible. Perhaps you think it will make you happy, too. But as you may have figured out by now, it won't make a difference unless it is something that was always a part of your own vision for your life to begin with.

You've got to be clear on what you want. Without clarity—there can be no success unless you stumble upon it by chance. Knowing what you desire and committing to pursuing it will get you what you want, in any facet of life.

In other words, you've got to be all in or you're all out. You are either invested 100% in your journey, or else you'll give it a mild try instead of taking definitive action.

Many people around you will go through life knowing what they do not want, but never figuring out exactly what they do want, and the price they're willing to pay to get there. In fact, when you listen to most people complaining, are they not griping about the things they don't want and the stuff they don't like and how they wish they didn't have to deal with this or that. Yet, these same people rarely know what they do want.

As Rhonda Byrne, the bestselling author of *The Secret,* has said: *"If you would only focus on what you wanted, that's all you would ever get."*

This flip in our thinking needs clarity to work. With clarity comes focus and a vision of how to get there.

With a "No Punches Pulled" approach to life, you will learn exactly how to use your creative prowess and your analytical aptitude to get to the root of what you want and why. You'll pursue your biggest dreams with laser-focused attention. And you will win—not because you have what it takes, but rather, because you're *willing to do whatever it takes* to succeed.

Whatever it takes. This is a powerful mantra to adopt right now. When you wake up every morning, and before you go to sleep, repeat this mantra to yourself. Say it out loud: *"I know exactly what I want, and I'm ready to do whatever it takes to get it."*

Building the Foundations of Clarity

Ready to get more clarity? Great! The good news—you don't need to *find* clarity. You get to *build* it. It's a choice. You get to decide what you want. You have to look within yourself to understand why you want what you do. You have to stop waiting around for inspiration to strike, or luck to favor you. You've got to sit down today and decide that you'll bring to reality whatever you wish to have.

Tom Bilyeu of *Impact Theory* has said: "Power is closing your eyes, visualizing a world you want, and building it."

Clarity is that process where you get to determine what exactly it is that you truly desire. And later, the process for building it as you gear up for doing whatever it takes to make it.

Perhaps you've spent years going down a particular career path hoping there will be an exit into something you love. Perhaps you're stuck in a rut with regard to a relationship and waiting to see what course it takes. Maybe you've grown used to blaming others. You might be waking up every morning, hoping and praying that today is the day when something changes.

But how long are you willing to go down a path that you've already realized is not meant for you? How long are you willing to wait before you consciously switch gears? How long will you let the clinging difficulties of your past and present eat away at your desired future?

Only you can steer yourself back on track, and to do so, you need to build change into your life.

Change—like clarity—must be an intentional choice. Clarity without intention becomes confusion. Confusion leads to indecision and frustration. When you know what it is you're going for, the decisions you must make to get there are clearly defined. You're making intentional choices as opposed to being pulled around by vague ideas and someone else's plan.

As Jim Rohn once said: "If you don't design your own life plan, chances are you'll fall into someone else's plan. And guess what they have planned for you? Not much.

You want to start taking total ownership of your life, and committing to sit with your most difficult thoughts to build a clear picture for your future, one that stems from your values and builds a clear vision of what you want the most.

Imagine this: It's ten years from now. Where do you want to be? Who do you want to become? What set of specific actions must you take today, tomorrow and all the days moving forward to begin moving toward this vision? Spend time reflecting on this and write down as clear a description as you can.

Don't worry about commitment right now. Don't overthink anything. Don't worry about keeping your options open, or about diversifying your risks. At least not yet. Step one is just about finding the answer to one simple question—what exactly do you want out of your life? Decide, and write it out. If you don't know, write down anything just to get started.

Greater Clarity Today Starts the Journey

Clarity will help you make better decisions and choices. Without it, your life will continue to be haphazard. Sometimes wonderful, sometimes gloomy, but not steered consciously by you in one direction. Take it from me, you don't want to wake up someday in your old age spending your last few days on Earth wondering what your life could have been like if only you had taken action, or made a decision, or had been less scared to do anything.

By reading this book and implementing the **No Punches Pulled** framework, you won't have to fear ending up in *that* situation. You will be in total charge of your life and living the dream instead of dreaming about living.

It's possible that your present reality does not reflect your dream future—it doesn't need to. It's up to you to make the journey, and to make it a beautiful one. You will need to pause, reflect and evaluate where you are from time to time. You'll need to build more knowledge and learn as you go. You will need to pivot and change direction when you get off course. You will need to reach out to those who can support and amplify your vision.

But when you're making all your decisions from a place of clarity, and in the direction of a clear vision, you'll make decisions that are on point. What's more, you'll be confident in making them. You'll stand behind what you've chosen. You'll grow from strength to strength, with each win stacking onto the other.

There's no doubt that there will be distractions begging for your attention. The idea is to know where you're headed, so that any breaks or minor detours are conscious choices, knowing that you'll be back to work shortly.

The wisest philosophers and most successful business people on the planet repeatedly say that the secret to your future lies in your present. So, for a better tomorrow, build clarity today, wasting no more time on mistakes and failures of the past.

Know Why People Want What They Want

In your quest to build clarity on what you want, it might be helpful for you to know why it's likely for you to want certain things. Where do these needs and desires come from? Why are some needs more compelling than others? Why do you outgrow some of them? What does real fulfillment look like?

You're more likely to find a lot of these answers if you understand the six basic human needs that we all have in common.

The six human needs are:

- **Love** – a need for an emotional connection with others
- **Growth** – a need to expand and elevate yourself
- **Significance** – a need to feel important and cherished
- **Contribution** – a need to be able to offer something to others
- **Certainty** – a need for assurance and safety
- **Variety** – a need for exposure to the unknown and exciting

These needs are deep-seated and drive each of our choices, whether we make them consciously or subconsciously. Everyone is naturally unique and shaped by a distinct set of beliefs, circumstances and mindset. But, by understanding the fundamental categories of our needs, we're more likely to be able to articulate them better to build more clarity about what we want to dedicate our lives to.

Now that you know the importance of building clarity in your present to arrive at the future of all your big dreams, it's time to build laser focus clarity.

Your NPP Laser-Focus Clarity Formula

This chapter has been about knowing exactly what you want, so that you can get started and begin moving in the right direction. Your NPP formula shows you exactly how to build this clarity, because without it, you'll fall back into old patterns of uncertainty, doubt and the fear of failure.

You won't have all the answers now, and that is OK, but as you continue to push ahead, more of the details will show up for you. It's a process of continuous growth.

The **clarity formula** asks you to follow five simple steps.

(1) Know your "why"

Knowing exactly why you want something is what creates your drive. It's likely that your goals are big and scary, as they should be. If you're driven by a powerful "why," you're more apt to stay on course when things get hard.

And, **the only guarantee is that the way will be hard.**

Every person has a "why"; it's just that they may not clearly know what it is. Some people struggle to admit what their big why is for fear of being ridiculed.

Remember—your "why" is only for you; it is to help you build and maintain laser-focus clarity. You don't have to justify it to anyone else. Your why leads to purpose, and purpose leads to building out the foundations of a fulfilling life.

Here is what you need to do: Write down your "why." How will getting what you want ultimately create the lifestyle you really want? What lies beneath your desire to hit that goal? How will accomplishing it make you feel? Why won't you give up? What is the purpose that fuels you? What are the consequences if you don't live into your WHY? What do you stand to lose if you don't succeed?

Knowing what you want is critical. But also, knowing the consequences of giving up and buying into confusion will lead to the worst situation imaginable—future regret.

Defining your *why* is the driver to creating an unbreakable obsession to make it.

(2) Articulate your mission

Oscar Wilde once said, "Appearance blinds, whereas words reveal."

Finding the words to capture your dreams and vision, and writing down your mission with definitive certainty, can be an empowering and rewarding practice. Not only does it force you to take your dreams seriously, converting them from something vaguely imagined to a vision deliberately articulated, but the simple act of writing reinforces clarity. You can't write a goal down in one clear sentence unless you know exactly what you want.

Writing your goal clearly makes all the difference between a wish and a plan—you aren't asking the universe for something but, rather, confirming what you want—and subsequently—how you're going to get it.

To make this practice even more powerful, once you've written down your goal, rewrite it frequently in the form of an affirmation, in the present tense, as though you've already accomplished your goal.

Affirmations help you stay focused on what you want and keep you repeating the positive and not the negative aspects of your goal. Further, the present tense builds a sense of urgency. There's a big difference between saying "I will earn a million dollars in annual fees someday" and "I am earning a million dollars in fees by the end of 2022."

Right now, put pen to paper (and do so repeatedly), signaling to your mind at both a conscious and subconscious level, what your exact plan is.

Do this practice every morning for the next thirty days as soon as you wake up. Don't touch your phone. Don't fall into the trap of worrying about your problems. Before you go to bed, put out a notepad and a pen, on your desk in plain view, and when you get up, take five minutes to breathe. Then, for ten minutes, write out your dreams and desires.

(3) Make your goals specific, objective, and quantifiable

A big impediment to building clarity is setting vague goals. "I want to be rich" is not a goal, it is a wish. "A billion dollars in net worth by 2030" is a goal. It's important that you make your goals specific and measurable, so that you know what you're pursuing, how far from it you are at any given point in time, and whether you've achieved it or not. Even in cases where your goals are about things more general or subjective in nature, you must adapt a form of measurability to track your progress.

For example, if your goal is to improve your skills as a photographer, take stock of where you stand now—you could grade yourself (perhaps currently a "C"?), put a specific date by which you'll be at a "B," and one by which you'll be at an "A+."

You want to make things clear with bright lines so that you stay fixed on the process of moving forward; it's time to stop making excuses and stop living in the "gray zone."

The gray zone is for people who are still uncertain, not committed, and are on the fence about what they want. They try a few things and give up, convincing themselves that it didn't work.

Right now, set your goal and create the first three action tasks you intend to take this week to move forward with this goal. There are no excuses when you know what you truly want.

(4) Be deliberate with your commitment

Without practice, there can be no progress. The same is true of everything you do, whether it's training in the martial arts or goal setting and building more clarity.

- You want to practice your affirmations every day.

- You want to visualize your dreams every day.

- You want to write down your exact goals, and;

- your detailed plan to reach your outcome.

Daily practices are powerful and integral to building momentum and mastery. It doesn't matter what your goal is—you have to find a way to reinforce your goal and your efforts toward it every single day.

If you want to become a better writer, write every day. If you want to build a healthy relationship, show kindness and gratitude to your partner every day. If you want to be more fit, work out or eat better every day.

To build complete clarity, integrate your goals as a part of your daily focus until you refine, live, and breathe them, and see how much more you begin to love the dream you're building.

In the words of Blaise Pascal: "Clarity of mind means clarity of passion, too; this is why a great and clear mind loves ardently and sees distinctly what it loves."

(5) Follow up with aligned action

No amount of affirmation, visualization or goal setting will be helpful unless it is followed up with massive action. Clarity will drive action, and the converse is also true—the more actions you take, the more you can refine your goals, and in doing so, build a better plan with detailed clarity.

You don't want to treat your goals (or the practice of goal setting) as a onetime and unchangeable endeavor. You want to make your goals a part of you—they become more refined as you grow.

Actions aligned with your path help you set a clearer vision, and are more informed by facts and experience. Even when you make a mistake, you've learned something you didn't previously know, and it will strengthen your resolve to get to your target from a place of trial and error. This is called learning, and you can only learn from your mistakes when you accept them and push forward no matter what.

No action—or random acts not aligned with a clear path—can keep you stuck in a rut or take you toward a destination you don't want to be. But consistent action in the direction of your ultimate goal will get you there one way or another.

In time, your months and years of hard, consistent work will pay off in massive dividends. The greatest investment you can make is in yourself and your dreams.

Chapter takeaways

- Knowing what you want, why you want it, and the price you're willing to pay to get it is imperative for success; without clarity, you'll find it harder to pursue your goals and stay focused.
- Clarity is not to be found, but rather to be built. It requires deliberate effort, and a commitment to a specific path.

- Clarity is a necessity for making better decisions; it keeps you from getting lost indefinitely.
- Understanding your fundamental human needs can help you build more clarity, as you will know where your desires stem from.
- The formula to build laser-focused clarity involves knowing your "why," committing your vision to paper, making your goals as specific as possible, practicing a commitment to clarity, and following up with consistent, massive action over a long period of time.
- Never give up. Pivot and shift your course when you find yourself blocked.

"*Failure should be our teacher, not our undertaker. Failure is delay, not defeat. It is a temporary detour, not a dead end. Failure is something we can avoid only by saying nothing, doing nothing, and being nothing.*"

— **Denis Waitley**

Throw Away Plan B
(and go all in)

"Life is inherently risky. There is only one big risk you should avoid at all costs, and that is the risk of doing nothing."

Denis Waitley

Growing up, you're likely to have heard, *"don't put all your eggs in one basket."* Perhaps you still have people telling you to *"always have a backup plan."* While people have good intentions with this advice, most people are risk-averse and believe in hedging against uncertainties.

Most people like to have a cushion to fall back on. Most people don't like to fail. Having a backup plan makes handling the failure easier. And that's exactly where the problem with having a backup plan is.

But let me ask you this: Why would you want to make it easier for yourself to fail?

Your plan A is what you *really* want. It's your dream. It's what keeps you up at night. It represents the best of what you want to achieve, have, do, or be. Plan B (and plans C and D if you have them) are next to best; they're your way of telling yourself, *"Oh well, this is also good ..."* But it isn't. You know it isn't. And it will only become clearer to you in the long run.

This book is showing you how to pursue, win, drive and thrive at your absolute best, "No Punches Pulled" level of relentless obsession to beat all obstacles standing between you and everything else. Second best simply won't do.

Removing Self Doubt and Your Escape Hatch

Plan A is the only plan if you want to succeed. It requires that you go all in. There's no room for doubt, second-guessing your actions, clinging to the fear of failure, or being afraid to lose. There's no way to escape because you trust that you won't need to. And that's why there's no room for plan B.

If you have a plan B, I'm suggesting that you throw it out *now*. Why? It's a signal to your brain that, if you fall, something will be there to catch you. There is a safety net. It's not a backup plan for if you fail, but when you do, because by creating a backup plan, it holds you back from going all in.

To become a top performer, a master, a leader, or someone that wants to make dreams happen, you must be all in with your plan. Having a backup plan is like building an escape route for when it all falls to pieces. You're planning to fail before you even take one step forward.

It keeps you making half-hearted attempts

When you know you have a backup plan, your back is not against the wall. You know that even if you don't give your 100%, it's going to be alright because you have a safety net. Throw away plan B, and you have no more excuses for half-hearted efforts.

It gives you permission to quit

Let's say you've been doing your absolute best, but you hit a roadblock (which everyone always does). When you only have one path ahead of you with no room for a U-turn and no options for a detour, you're going to figure out a way to keep going, aren't you?

Get rid of plan B, and you have no permission to quit. If you do, you'll have nowhere to go. You have no choice but to figure out how to overcome your obstacle. Your *might do* becomes a *must do*.

It keeps you from listening to your true self

Plan A aligns with your values and your dreams. But when you make a plan B, you are feeding into your fears and false security.

At best, plan B is a diluted version of what you really want out of your life, and at worst, it's completely divorced from your true desires. There's a reason you built plan A. It came from your heart, your intuition. Throw away plan B simply because it will keep you from listening to your true self.

It diverts your time and energy

Imagine you're an entrepreneur. You're up against the odds, you're short on time, and you're juggling various stakeholders, from consumers to investors to vendors. It's hard work. You need all of your time, strength and resources to make it work, but in parallel, you're trying to keep a plan B running as well, just in case. In most cases, attempts to have both plan A and plan B afloat will cause both to suffer.

Each of us, from the most modest to the wealthiest, has limited resources, whether these are in the form of money, time, mental bandwidth, energy, health, or emotional capacity. When you're focused on one path ahead of you, on one all-consuming vision, you're dedicating 100% of your resources to it. When you make a plan B, you're splitting your resources, diverting your time, your money, or your energy. Don't do it.

Create a plan and follow your blueprint, pivoting as you go, but always pushing forward with relentless pursuit.

It makes you hazy and lazy

Say you're at a job you hate, but you're sticking around because it's your plan B; you're resisting starting your own venture or jumping ship to get that job you really love because plan B isn't so bad after all. Yes, maybe your work environment is toxic, but the money is fair. Yes, you haven't learned anything new in a while, but hey—at least you get that free pizza on Fridays.

Do this long enough—and you'll find you've stopped following (or even knowing) your own values and goals, and forgotten about the kind of person, professional or entrepreneur you wanted to be.

Plan B can make you hazy; it can get you comfortable at the cost of what you truly want. Take that leap of faith and cut the cord to your backup—it's now or never. Chase what you love to do with all you've got, take breaks when you need to, but don't lose sight of your real goals.

Kill your laziness before it kills you. Get clear on your priorities and dig in for the long ride.

It doesn't force you to get creative

You've quit that "safety" job? Great! Now you need to figure out how you're going to make money doing what you love. You've finally ended that relationship that wasn't really bringing you happiness?

It's time to introspect so that you can become more centered in yourself. How are you going to do this? It's time to explore ways to heal and meet new people. When you don't have a plan B, you're forced to get creative, and this will *always* lead to something wonderful in time.

So, though plan A may be the hard way out, you want to make sure it's the *only* way out. If you want to take the island, you must burn your ships; once you've got no way to retreat, you're going to have to be 100% committed.

Your Backup Plan Reality Check

Now you're ready to totally immerse yourself in building a plan A mindset. Here's a quick reality check that will tell you where you currently stand, and make it easier for you to face your fears and doubts as you filter it out of your plan.

Note your thoughts on the below questions:

What is your plan A?

How much do you trust in your plan A?

Do you have a plan B? If yes, what is it?

Why did you (really) make a plan B?

What's the worst that can happen if there's no plan B?

From here on, you're deciding to overcome the fear that's keeping you tied up with plan B. Your task now is to focus entirely on plan A. You're going to remove plan B from your mind; when it appears, you know that it is just your fear calling to you, and that you aren't going to give in to it.

Removing Plan B from the Equation

Getting rid of plan B becomes easier if you've done all you can to ensure you don't need it in the first place. You can take certain specific steps that will make it easier for you to stop depending on backups. Once you've done this, it's time to remove your doubt and uncertainty. When it crops up, there are 5 steps you can take to ensure you don't get pulled off course.

Here are 5 steps to show you how:

Step 1 – Think carefully about what you really want, and once you've decided, commit to it. Go All In 100%.

Once you've put in the time and the work to introspect and learn about what you really want and why, you're more likely to be able to commit to it entirely, at the cost of all else. You want to be so completely in love with what you want that your mind doesn't accept any excuses and backups.

Naturally, there's no need then for a plan B. No distractions. No room for mediocrity. And no stopping until you've won.

Step 2 – Reallocate your resources and strengthen your plan A strategy

It's likely that your backup plan has taken up some of your resources. Maybe you've set aside some money—you can now channel that back into plan A. You never know—it might just give you the opportunity to take that one make-or-break extra step. Stop allowing plan B to block the resources you need for plan A.

Step 3 – Embrace your fear and let it motivate you

You're throwing away plan B—does that mean you expect there to be no setbacks as you go all out on plan A? Of course not! If you're chasing something big, there will be obstacles. You will get scared. You will even be terrified from time to time. But the best part is— embracing your fear can also be your biggest motivator.

For instance, if you've got to build your dream company (plan A) now that you don't have your "safety" job (plan B), you're pushed to make it work because you've got to have a roof over your head and food on your table.

Your fear was keeping you stuck to plan B—now that there is no plan B, you'll be fueled to complete what you set out to do as part of plan A, no matter what. The idea isn't to be careless or delusional; it is to anticipate the seriousness of the challenge ahead and face it head-on.

Step 4 – Build a support system

A support system here doesn't mean people who will write you checks; it's an ecosystem of cheerleaders and advisors. It's about having family, friends or a mentor who can keep you on your path to plan A.

You want people to remind you of your strengths and to be honest with you about your weaknesses. You want all the support you can get to maximize your chances for your shot at plan A.

At work, you want to encourage a culture of support, so that your colleagues are committed to their own plan A's instead of trying to mitigate their risks and hiding their failures with plan B's.

Step 5 – Learn to manage risks better

As you throw away plan B and get ready to go full steam on plan A, remember that taking calculated risks is very different from being reckless. The more you can foresee the threats you're likely to face, the better you can plan for them. This is your responsibility to yourself as well as to others as a leader.

Know that you will need to course correct. Know that you will need to manage setbacks. It doesn't mean you're failing at plan A; it just means you need to get better at anticipating risks.

Chapter takeaways

- By building a plan B, you're making it easier for yourself to fail at plan A.

- Get rid of plan B; it's keeping you from doing your best and from listening to your true self, giving you permission to quit, diverting your resources, making you hazy about your values and preventing you from unleashing your creative best.

- Think about why you feel the need to make your plan B in the first place. Be honest with yourself in terms of what you're afraid of. Identify your fears acting a shackles holding you in place. Write down this fear now. Then, take the paper, ball it up, and throw it in the trash.

- Commit 100% to your plan A. Re-channel your resources, embrace your fears, build a support system, and learn how to get better at anticipating and mitigating risks. This will make it easier for you to stop depending on backups.

Go to War with Your Mind
(Every Morning)

"It all begins and ends in your mind.
What you give power to has power over you."

Leon Brown

Everything that unfolds in YOUR life first comes alive within you. Your reality begins and ends with your own mind. Your thoughts determine your feelings, inform your choices, and guide your actions.

In the words of Buddha, *"What you think, you become."*

Your battle then, is not with the world around you, but the world within you—the world that your mind is creating and recreating every second of every day. It's you and only you that is responsible for your outer reality, and that depends on your inner world.

While many of us understand this, we keep taking our mind for granted. Instead of nourishing it, we abuse it. Instead of understanding it, we ignore it. We overlook the remarkable power and malleability of our minds. We waste the potential we can unlock with it, while the biggest achievers in the world use it day after day as their most potent weapon.

This book is teaching you how to go all out and hold nothing back. And you can't do this unless you learn how to control your mind (especially when it wants to control you instead).

You can't get better at controlling your mind by numbing the chaos with pointless distractions such as social media, television, comfort food, or alcohol. And neither do you want to expend all of your energy every day in fighting your mind and breaking yourself against its defense mechanisms.

If you want to win the war against your own mind, and against the world outside you, you have to learn how to make your mind bulletproof.

Before you learn the techniques to develop a bulletproof mind, it's important you know exactly what it means to have one. Your mind is a reservoir of your experiences, knowledge, thoughts, values and beliefs about yourself and your world.

There are countless distractions you will encounter every day. There are myriad pieces of information that will be thrown your way, whether you're consuming these consciously or subconsciously. There's a barrage of thoughts that will be generated in your mind; some will just pass by, others will stick, and yet others will provoke an emotional or physical response.

Building a bulletproof mind is about training yourself to filter the information you allow into your mind. It's about learning what to react to, and what to simply let go, without an emotional response. It's about staying true to your beliefs and centered within yourself. A bulletproof mind will keep you from getting swayed by irrelevant information or energy shifts occurring in the world outside you all the time.

You have to learn exactly how to strengthen your mind a little more each day. Will it take work? Yes. Will it be worth it? You can't even begin to imagine.

8-Step Battle Plan to Building a Bulletproof Mind

Here's how you can begin intentionally building a bulletproof mind by focusing on creating a fortified mental protection system.

#1 – Ask yourself the difficult questions

As you get to work on your battle plan, begin by being completely honest with yourself. Do you have what you want? Are you on the path you want to be on? Are you certain you will achieve your goals? Spend some time digging in and uncovering the real blocks that are holding you back.

- Why don't you have the kind of relationship you really want?
- Why aren't you living in your dream home? Or driving the car you like the most?
- Why don't you have enough money?
- Why aren't you building your dream business?
- Why aren't your relationships with your family and friends thriving?
- Why isn't your health in order?

Only you can answer these questions for yourself. To unleash the best of your mind's potential, start by throwing out all excuses and being totally honest with yourself.

#2 – Release your past and the beliefs that are holding you back

One of the toughest struggles you'll face is releasing the limiting beliefs holding you back, and a lot of these are likely to have come about from your past experiences. Many limiting beliefs come from our childhood and, we aren't even sure of patterns of imprinting and conditioning we've been subjected to through the decades.

Uncovering these will take a ton of work, but once you've completely broken away from these limiting beliefs, you'll feel like a weight you've carried around for months, years or decades has been lifted, leaving you with a surge of wonderful energy.

Passively accepting things the way they are by telling yourself, "that's how life works" or "that's just how it is" is going to get you nowhere. You need to examine, identify, and exterminate beliefs that are harming your future. You want to do this as often as you need to in your endeavor to strengthen your mind. It will take time, but the results you achieve will always be dependent upon the amount of focus and work invested into the process.

One critical reminder: the point here is to not dive into your past and get wrapped up in past drama of everything that happened to you and who did what and why. Your goal is to focus on what you can change, and not try to figure out the past.

By staying true to the course moving forward—the only direction that matters—you can move away from past trauma and close the gap between where you are now, who you want to be, and what you will ultimately transition into when you get there.

#3 – Make sure that the future you're chasing is aligned with your values

Bruce Lee once said, "The successful warrior is the average man, with laser-like focus." Unless you know exactly what you want and why, you aren't going to have a laser-like focus. Try to zero in on exactly what you want out of your future. It doesn't matter where you find yourself today; start afresh, start now, start here.

What is your biggest dream or goal? Is it to…

- become a multi-millionaire?
- solve the world's energy crisis?
- have the most loving family in the world?
- buy a dream house on an island (and you love it so much you buy the island too)?
- send your children to a particular school?

Now try to articulate exactly *why* you want these things. How do these goals line up with the values that matter most to you in life? Where are these desires coming from? Your heart, your mind, or because others expect them from you? What does your gut tell you? How do you want to give purpose to your one and only life? Let your dream future be a product of the values that matter most to you, and make sure your "why" is coming from your authentic self.

Having your "what" and your "why" at the top of your mind fuels you and keeps your mind focused. It pulls your thinking toward your dreams. With such a powerful pull, trust that you'll figure out the "how."

#4 – Feed your mind only with the best

The most successful people in the world know that knowledge, like money, compounds over time. They commit to learning something new every day. They feed their minds only with the best information.

To build a bulletproof mind, you have to become very cognizant of the information you're consuming, how worthwhile it is, how accurate it is, and how helpful it is to you at this stage of your life.

Ask yourself how much time you spend on social media, and what good comes from it. Ask yourself when you last signed up for an online course or watched a TED talk. Ask yourself how you last applied something new you had recently learned.

We live in an age of information overload. It's your job to separate the inflow into what's harming you and what's helping you, and into what's irrelevant to you and what's exactly aligned with your needs.

#5 – Choose the right mentors

Absolutely everything you're trying to do has already been done. Even if you're working on a novel, disruptive, one-of-a-kind business model, there are people who have faced and overcome challenges of a similar nature.

Having a mentor can be one of the best things you can do to shape your mindset and to keep yourself on the right track. Why not learn from the masters? Why not save time avoiding the mistakes they've made? Why not learn from those who have similar values? All you've got to do is reach out.

#6 – Block out the naysayers

With all the work you're doing to feed your mind with the best information and the most helpful guidance, to make it truly bulletproof, you want to guard your mind by keeping out the negativity. You need to protect yourself not only against the skeptics and the envious, but also from incorrect information and triggers of emotional breakdowns.

You are responsible first and foremost to your own self, and you can't build the life of your dreams if you're constantly putting yourself amid negativity. So, keep out the naysayers. Spend the majority of your time with the top-level performers in your field. You have no time or mental energy for time wasters or life bashers.

The measure of your progress will always be measured by the people you choose to engage with, regardless if it's a 1-1 conversation or virtually. It's not only what you focus on that matters, but who you focus on. Listen to the words and wisdom of great philosophers and leaders who are living the life you want to lead.

#7 – Visualize your dream every day

One of the best ways to channel your energy toward your goals and keep your mind focused is by visualizing your dream each day. Imagine you've already achieved what you want. What does that look like? What does that feel like?

Imagine every detail of your dream, as accurately and vividly as you can. The more you visualize your dream, the stronger your pull toward it will be. Your desire will enable your mind to function at its best.

#8 – Exercise daily to keep your mind alert

The last step in your battle plan to build a bulletproof mind is the most underestimated, but one of the most powerful ways to boost your mental strength. Exercising your body and your mind every day can compound, bringing you clarity and results that will leave you astounded.

Whether you prefer aerobic exercise or yoga, a workout is the best way to recharge your body as well as your mind. And meditating daily will keep you centered, focused and positive through your toughest days.

Follow the strategies in this battle plan again and again, and you'll keep winning the war against your mind.

Chapter takeaways

- Remember that your external reality is determined by your internal world. You build your future first and foremost in your mind.

- Your mind can be unimaginably powerful when its fullest potential is unleashed. But more often than not, we take our mind for granted, abusing and ignoring its capacity.

- A bulletproof mind is a mind that is trained to filter information; it knows what to react to, and what to simply let go. It drives important actions and isn't shaken up with irrelevant information or energy shifts in the world outside.

- To build a bulletproof mind, be honest with yourself. Identify and release the beliefs that are holding you back, commit to your future, visualize it daily, learn as much as you can from others, block out the negativity and exercise your body and your mind.

- Spend the majority of your time with positive thinkers and action takers. Absorb the wisdom of the ages and create relationships with game changers

Accelerate Your Standards
(and raise everything by 1000%)

"Create the highest, grandest vision possible for your life, because you become what you believe."

Oprah Winfrey

The standards you set for your life form the basis of all your achievements. You will become what you set out to become and you will and up with everything you target to have. Your standards form a guide for your choices and set the bar for the actions that you will hold yourself accountable for.

Setting high standards and honoring them over and over will increase your confidence, bring you success, and have the right people and opportunities come to you. Never be afraid to set the highest of standards, and don't worry about justifying these to the people around you. The higher the standards you set, the more you will end up elevating your life, whether that's the quality of your health, relationships, work, or finances. And this will be more and more visible with time. So don't worry about *telling* people, *show* them.

Most people don't realize that the standards they have set for themselves are limited by and dependent on how they grew up. Every individual absorbs what goes on in their environment and becomes conditioned to the beliefs of others. They set standards for themselves as children, based on what they see in their peers.

The good news? These standards are not set in stone. Who you are and what you identify with are not fixed. You can change this now, if you wish to. Only you can decide what you want and what you deserve, and in truth this has got nothing to do with your past or what you have accomplished so far. So, go on, raise the bar to what many would call "impossible," and commit to jumping over it.

If you need inspiration, think of the African American high jumper Cornelius Cooper Johnson. As an eighteen-year-old, he was awarded fourth place in the high jump at the 1932 Olympics despite having cleared the same height as the three winners. Undeterred, Johnson went on to win several AAU championships in subsequent years and made an Olympic record leap at six feet eight inches at the 1936 Berlin Olympics.

He achieved all he did while battling widespread racism; Hitler is said to have left the Olympic stadium so as to avoid meeting him, and Roosevelt reportedly refused to host him at the White House. Johnson taught us how to set and overcome standards deemed impossible without making excuses and blaming others.

It's your turn to elevate your game. The best way to elevate your life? Raise the bar. Reset your expectations. Analyze what you think you deserve in each important area of your life and why you think you only deserve that much. All around, you're likely to see people stuck at low paygrades or in unfulfilling relationships because that's what they believe they deserve. That's what they believe is the best they can do.

If you tell yourself it's OK to settle, and to be mediocre, guess what? That's where you're going to stay. And if you tell yourself that you deserve nothing but the absolute best in every aspect of life that matters to you, and you'll demand excellence no matter what, that's where you're going to go.

In the words of Ruskin Bond, *"Life will always give us what we are worth. It never fails to take us at our own valuation."* What do you think you're worth?

Your primer to helping you set your highest standards

Here are 10 highly effective strategies to help you reset your internal narrative and boldly set the highest standards for the life of your dreams. You can choose the ones that resonate the most with you or follow all for maximum impact.

#1. Decide what you deserve

You and only you, free from all influences and conditioning, must decide what you feel you are worth. Whether it's a certain amount of money, an executive position at a dream firm, or a one-of-a-kind relationship, or all three—*you* get to decide what you deserve.

Once you've done this, look at your goals closely. Now raise the bar tenfold. Set the highest standards possible for your life. You will achieve them. All you've got to do to begin is to believe in yourself.

#2. Build self-discipline

This book is showing you how to seriously level up in a way you never imagined you could. You've built clarity around your dreams, and you believe you deserve them. To get there, a key ingredient is discipline. Discipline will complement your desire. It will get you through the days where your motivation fizzles out and when there are no cheerleaders around.

Many productivity experts maintain that self-discipline is the hardest and yet most important form of self-love. Stop giving in to every distraction or temptation. Stop eating junk food, indulging in self-sabotage, living in the past, or living under the weight of what others expect. You're answerable to yourself for how your life turns out, and you're gifting yourself your future by building a disciplined mind and life.

#3. Stay on top of your finances

We live in a world where everything we do costs money. Unless you're in a financially secure position, you're going to struggle to chase the best that you want out of your life. It's harder to take a plunge into a risky entrepreneurial venture if you've got a ton of credit card debt. It's harder to surprise your spouse with that weekend in Paris if you still owe money to your neighbor.

As you set out to raise your standards 1000%, begin by getting on top of money matters, and into the habit of staying on top of them. You'll be surprised at the security, freedom, and energy you feel once you're no longer struggling financially.

#4. Stop lying to yourself

It's great to feel happy with the goals you've set for yourself, but ensure you aren't lying to yourself with what you feel is "good enough." The first step to getting anything or anywhere is by owning that you want it.

To stop lying to yourself, you may need to really dig in deep to get to the cause of why you had set the standards you had in the past. Your belief system and sense of self-worth are complex composites of your attitudes, abilities, and influences.

To set and chase standards that are 1000% higher than what you initially believed you deserved, you'll need to change your narrative. In the words of Tony Robbins, to raise the standard for your life, turn "shoulds" into "musts." Refuse to accept anything less than your ultimate goals.

#5. Stop settling

Stop letting yourself off the hook for settling, whether it's in terms of your salary or the quality of your friendships. Settling at work can be fatal. We wouldn't have Apple if Steve Jobs had settled. We wouldn't have the *Mona Lisa* if Leonardo Da Vinci had settled. We wouldn't have *Harry Potter* if J. K. Rowling had settled.

Commit to never settling. Commit to elevating your game each day, and those of everyone around you will follow. Keep raising the bar. Keep winning. Keep expecting the best of the best. You will get it. If it takes time, let it. It will be worth it.

#6. Remind yourself of the cost of failing (to live up to your standards)

If you're scared to raise your standards, shift perspective and ask yourself, "What if I commit to something that is far below my fullest potential? What if I fail to have what I dream of because I refuse to raise my standards and raise my game?" I promise you. That it's much scarier to think along these lines.

There is a cost for not elevating your life while you still have the capacity to do it. You're failing to break beyond your self-imposed limitations. Explain to yourself the pain you will feel in the future if you stay within these imaginary limits. Be brave now—your future self will thank you for it.

#7. Talk kindly and positively to yourself

When you've had a difficult past, it can be extremely difficult to break a pattern of negative recurring thoughts. It can be hard to be kind to yourself and to others. Here's when you need to train your mind to adopt a positive internal dialogue, no matter how hard it may seem to do.

A good technique to get you started thinking positively is to remember (and to journal) your accomplishments and favorite experiences. Another is to find inspiration from other people like you, who have won, built, or earned what you want. Yet another is to spend more time with people who encourage you and help you achieve your goals. You want to fully believe, and repeatedly tell yourself, "I deserve all I want," "I can go out and get anything I set my mind to," and "I won't stop until I've met my goals."

It's only when you're talking to yourself in a manner that is encouraging and positive that you can expect the best from yourself and set your highest standards yet.

#8. Separate the critics from the cheerleaders

You know by now that you must guard your mindset and shut out the naysayers—the people who are constantly telling you that what you want is impossible, or that you don't deserve what you want. There are likely to be two more kinds of people around you—your critics and your cheerleaders. You'll need both of these.

Your critics will be honest with you and provide you with constructive feedback, helping you improve. And your cheerleaders will push you to go on in your darkest hours. Your cheerleaders can even be role models you follow who inspire you and help you raise your standards.

#9. Guard your boundaries in all their forms

Setting—and living up to—your standards will, from time to time, require you to say *no*. There's no way around it, and you shouldn't be looking for ways around it. Individuals committed to their future know that setting and respecting healthy boundaries is part of the journey. No matter how hard you try, you can't be everything to everyone.

You need to guard yourself and set your boundaries in all aspects of life. This includes establishing physical boundaries, for instance, by setting standards for your privacy and your body. It includes respecting your intellectual standards by keeping yourself away from those who insult or dismiss your opinions. It includes establishing sexual boundaries, by articulating what you are and are not comfortable with. It includes building emotional boundaries, ensuring your feelings are understood, respected and reciprocated.

You'll also need to set financial boundaries—maybe you need to stop allowing freeloaders to live off you. And lastly, you need to have social boundaries. Not everyone around you will be able to understand or keep up with you as you level up—and you don't need to worry.

The right people will see and admire you for what you are and what you become. When in doubt, remember this quote by Mandy Hale: *"Refuse to lower your standards to accommodate those who refuse to raise theirs."*

Your standards are yours to set, yours to stick to, and yours to protect. Raise your standards by 10%. Then, raise your standards 100%. And when that becomes too comfortable, take it up to 1000%. The only thing standing between you and everything you desire to be is the level of standards you decide to live by and scale up to.

#10. Begin to play the part *now*

You've set your standards. You're visualizing your future. You can feel as though it's already here. Next, you've got to begin to play the part, *now*.

Be the person with those standards *now*, not later. Keep at it, and one day, you'll see your future has arrived, simply because you've pulled it to yourself.

Chapter takeaways

- The standards you set for your life will determine the shape your future takes. You'll become what you believe you are worth, so think as big as you can and trust that you'll grow into it.

- Only you must decide what you are worth. Your standards are your own to set, to believe in, to stick to, and to protect. It has got nothing to do with others.

- To set your highest standards yet, begin by deciding what you deserve. Build the discipline to keep going on tough days. Clean up your finances, stop lying to yourself, stop settling, and stop letting people cross your boundaries. Remind yourself of the cost of not living by your standards. Be kind to yourself and surround yourself with constructive critics and cheerleaders.

- Begin to play the part of who you want to become *now*, and you'll find yourself growing into that person and into your dream future.

Implement the Habit of Deliberate Practice
(and outwork everyone)

"Success has to do with deliberate practice. Practice must be focused, determined, and in an environment where there's feedback."

Malcolm Gladwell

Make no mistake: Success takes work. People around you may be more talented, have more resources at their disposal, have unfair advantages working in their favor, or may simply get lucky very often; and you can still be more successful if you outwork them, with deliberate practice and an unwavering commitment to your goal.

When asked what made him different from other actors, Will Smith is reported to have said, *"You might have more talent than me. You might be smarter than me. You might be sexier than me. All of those things. But if we get on a treadmill together, there's two things: You're getting off first, or I'm going to die. It's really that simple. I will not be outworked. Period!"*

In the pursuit of success, everything else pales in the face of determination and effort. Success is hard. Change is hard. And a habit of intentional, deliberate practice, day after day, sets the champions apart from the amateurs.

Deliberate practice does not mean following trending productivity, lifestyle, or business hacks. It does not mean repeating things mindlessly because you saw someone else do it. It isn't the same as regular practice. What it does mean is conscious, focused, and systematic practice day after day to train yourself to get better at achieving an important and specific goal.

It's very easy to spot individuals committed to a life dedicated to their goals. You can see it in the way they spend each day. It's that young man with two-day shifts going to night school with a smile on his face. It's that athlete who trains and trains until she simply can't get her workout wrong. It's that executive who comes in early morning before everyone to practice presenting in a boardroom. It's that rising entrepreneur who wakes up at five in the morning to get some work done before her toddler wakes up.

Ask yourself: Are you one of these individuals? How can you become one of them? Do you understand what your success will ask of you? Do you take complete ownership of your journey? Can you fully grasp the implications of this? And are you willing to commit to a habit of deliberate practice for as long as it takes to smash your goals?

Don't lie to yourself. What's truly the best it can be, and what isn't?

It's very common for people to accept and come to terms with the way they find their lives. While satisfaction is necessary, it's very different from lying to yourself about your happiness.

When you assume something can't get better than it already is, because it would require too much effort or because things are best left as they've always been—that's resignation. Take an honest assessment of your life and the role you play in this world. What are you wholeheartedly grateful for? What's great but has room for improvement? And what do you need to turn upside down and completely revamp?

You cannot build a "No Punches Pulled" approach for a life of holistic success and happiness or dive into a habit of deliberate practice toward your goals if you passively accept things you aren't truly happy with.

Deliberate practice can be your biggest competitive advantage

You may have heard that, in the end, it's not the external world you must conquer but the world within. Your biggest competitor or enemy is not anyone around you, but who you were yesterday—that's who you have to defeat. And you can do this with repeated deliberate practice. This may very well end up becoming your biggest competitive advantage, for the simple reason that very few individuals are committed to their goals with such a passion, and therefore, are able to grow faster than anyone around.

Train your spirit, mind, and body for greater endurance, for bigger challenges, and for more creativity. Look around you. Look at the most successful person in any industry. It's not the person who is the most gifted. It's not the person with the most luck. It's not the person with an unfair advantage. While these things might help people win short-term battles, it certainly won't help them win the long war. The war will always be won by those obsessed with their goals and committed to an insane discipline and laser-focused, consistent action.

Know that success is an inside job

What's the difference between a person who does something because they must do it and because they want to do it? It's everything. When you want to do something, you'll give it your 100%. When you have to, you'll put in as much effort as you can get away with. Real success, and the discipline of repeated deliberate practice, does not come with half-hearted effort.

If you're finding it hard to give your 100%, it's perhaps because you're on the wrong path. When you truly care about becoming the very best, you won't be OK with giving up. And you'll devote yourself to accomplishing your goal, leaving no stone unturned, without anyone asking you to do so.

The 9-fold path to deliberate practice

Now that you're ready to build the discipline and habit of deliberate practice, here are nine potent strategies for you to choose from and implement right away. Focus on one strategy at a time, until it has become a part of your approach, and you'll find yourself becoming unbreakable.

#1 – Throw away the idea of your breaking point

You may have heard that the best way to break your fear of something is by facing it. You must do precisely the things you never thought you could.

Somewhere down the line, you may have begun to limit your own potential. Perhaps it arose from a lack of confidence triggered by a snarky comment from a relative or colleague. Perhaps it was self-generated, because of a mistake or one subpar performance.

To become a champion and to build a life leading to your goals with unrivaled discipline, you want to throw away any ideas you may have in your mind about your own limitations or breaking points. With training and with time, you can break out of any comfort zone and push any boundary.

You're learning how to do this sensibly, systematically, and sustainably. You're learning how to take deliberate action from a place of clarity.

#2 – Work on improving your skills by 1% every day

We often set massive goals, try taking big leaps to get to them, and give up once our enthusiasm fizzles out. Deliberate practice involves a different approach; it's about focusing on getting just 1% better each day and knowing that the results will compound.

Today, with the world changing at a faster pace than ever before, even the brightest minds need to invest time in upskilling every day and brushing up on the latest advancements and technologies, or soon they'll find they've become extinct. Build a lesson plan to get better at your craft, trade, or knowledge and make a commitment to growing, by 1%, one day at a time, day after day.

Want to revamp your wardrobe? Try out or toss out one outfit each day. Want to become an excellent cook? Make one new item for breakfast each morning. Want to get stronger? Do one more push-up each workout. Save ten dollars each day. Wake up ten minutes earlier each day. Read ten pages of a book each day. Don't underestimate the power of small steps taken consistently in one direction.

#3 – Schedule one hour a day committed to your practice

No matter what goal you want to work toward, unless you carve out time for it in your daily schedule, you won't be able to work toward it with concentration and enthusiasm.

Be patient with yourself; you may find your mind wandering about for the first couple of days during your "practice hour," or you may find that it takes time for you to adapt to this new routine. It's a good idea to start with smaller time slots committed and move up until you're able to make the most out of a one-hour practice. You'll get there. Just keep at it.

#4 – Visualize your objective until it feels real

Visualization fuels a discipline of deliberate practice. When you can imagine—with every fiber of your body— what it feels like to win that championship, or to be on the cover of Forbes, or to laugh out loud with your one-year-old at her birthday, you'll be much more motivated to invest your effort and energy in that specific area of your life.

Visualize yourself as though you're already where you want to be, open your eyes to the present, and get cracking on your plan to get there.

#5 – Identify your distractions

You're imaginably surrounded by noise, both audible and visual. Distractions are everywhere. Everything screams for an instant reaction. We're habituated to instant gratification. We're losing patience. And at the same time, we're aware of the damage this is doing.

Say "no" to giving in to your distractions. Consciously choose what you give your time and energy to, physically, mentally and emotionally. Draw out your boundaries, and to build and maintain a life of deliberate practice in the direction of your dreams, stick to these boundaries. Remember, discipline is the strongest form of self-love.

#6 – Make your well-being a priority

If you aren't looking after yourself, if your physical and mental health isn't in order, no amount of success or wealth means anything. You want to get to your goals and the life of your dreams in a way that allows you to enjoy the fruits of your labor.

There's no reason why the journey itself shouldn't be enjoyable—in fact, it's imperative that it is. Make healthy living and joy an integral part of every day and you'll find more room for growth.

#7 – Understand your work rhythm and respond to it

Deliberate practice, focus and success require you to operate at your best. And for you to be able to do this, you need to give your body and mind time to rest and recuperate. Use whatever method works best for you, whether it's working in fixed slots of one to two hours and then taking a break, taking a midday break, waking up early to work, or working until late at night—you want to understand your body and mind's rhythms and work in alignment with them to be at your most efficient and productive self.

#8 – Admit when you're stuck

It's possible to get stuck in a rut. It's possible to hit a plateau. It's possible to reach a mental block or a writer's block. It's possible to get burned-out. There are many ways in which you could get stuck, and the first thing to do when this happens is to pause, realize, and admit it.

You may need a vacation. You may need a fresh perspective. You may need to shake some things up. Or you may need professional help—various solutions can help you move forward in your practice, if only you admit it.

#9 – Ask for support and accountability

In building a habit of deliberate practice, continuous learning and growth play a key role. You want to read as much as you can, listen to talks, and stay on top of what's happening in your industry or domain. Even with this, it is tough to make it to greatness without a cheerleader, advisor, or critic.

You need someone to push you. You need someone to keep you in check. And sometimes, you just need someone to listen to you. You can build a system of support and accountability in multiple ways—it could involve your family, friends, a coach, an accountability partner, a mentor, or a colleague. You could join groups to network with people building businesses similar to yours or sharing the same passions are you do.

Remember the words of Jim Rohn: "You're the average of the five people you spend most of your time with."

Chapter takeaways

- Outworking people with deliberate practice can help you triumph over others who may seem more talented or luckier. In the pursuit of success, nothing compares with sheer determination, effort, and discipline.

- To get better, resolve to never lie to yourself. Truly assess what is good, what is great, and what needs a complete revamp in your life or work.

- To build deliberate practice, you must throw away any preconceived notions of your breaking points and decide to improve by 1% each day. You must carve out practice hours dedicated to working on your goals.

- Visualize your objective until it feels real and silence your distractions.

- Take breaks when you need to; remember your well-being is top priority.

- Plan for long-term growth, admit when you're stuck so that you can find solutions, and get help from the best mentors and coaches in the world to build your best self yet.

To learn more about building the habit of deliberate practice, refer to my book _Undefeated_. Consider it a primer to show you how to master the odds stacked against you and take control of your destiny.

Understand Your Dark Side
(and Feed the Right Wolf)

"Until you make the unconscious conscious, it will direct your life and you will call it fate."

Carl Jung

You might have heard the story of a Cherokee chief and his grandson. The two were conversing about life, and the chief said that he had a fight going on within himself. It was a terrible fight between two wolves; one wolf was evil and embodied envy, guilt, greed, ego, lies and anger.

The other wolf stood for hope, joy, love, faith, truth, humility, and peace. He told his grandson that the same fight goes on within every person.

When the boy asked which wolf wins, the chief replied: *"The one you feed."*

This simple folk story captures an eternal and ubiquitous conflict in all humankind. There will always be two wolves within each individual. These wolves will be there in every aspect of their lives, whether it's their emotions or habits. There will always be a dark side and a light side.

This duality has been deeply studied in modern psychology. Carl Jung's work *Psychology and Religion* echoes this thesis and posits that every individual possesses qualities that their society has labeled as "undesirable," and, therefore, every individual fails to meet the impossible standards expected from him, leaving much suppressed within him.

We try to make up for what we think we lack by wearing more makeup, embarking on more rigorous diets, or working longer hours for more money. Some of us are more conscious of our "shortcomings" than others, but each of us carries a shadow, made of the desires and emotions that we have suppressed. It's our job to recognize both the light and the dark within us and try to learn from what each is trying to tell us and teach us.

You want to go all out and win everything you've ever dreamed of—that's why you're reading this book. You're likely to have learned from your life that there are many paths that can take you to where you want to go. Who you become depends on your mindset, which in turn is built by what you feed it.

Which side you feed is entirely up to you, and only you.

Both the light and the dark are equally powerful and can serve you to get to your goals. Both are, in many ways, necessary for your growth and success. But it's up to you to recognize both your wolves and choose the type of character you want to build. If you're a *Star Wars* fan, you'll remember Yoda's words to Luke: "*If once you start down the dark path, forever will it dominate your destiny.*"

In building your "No Punches Pulled" approach to life, you have to conquer your dark side. This doesn't mean you don't learn from it or listen to it—it just means you don't let it consume you. All the time, we see people blaming others or seeking revenge instead of addressing the trauma within them and trying to heal from it.

We see bright young people stuck in patterns of self-sabotage and self-harm. We see extraordinary winners with fantastic achievements destroy everything that led them to the heights of their success. We see the dark side win far too often. But it doesn't need to. It's time for you to learn how to face it, conquer it and wield it to your advantage.

Overcome Your Darkness: The NPP Edition

Here are 5 strategies to help you tackle your dark side, keep feeding the right wolf, and in doing so, build an unbreakable character over time.

#1. Acknowledge your dark side – don't suppress it

An interesting branch of psychology based on Jung's theories refers to "shadow work," which entails "making the unconscious conscious." Many of us are ignorant of our dark sides, but in truth, we all have negative qualities, and we tend to hide them.

We try to appear "perfect" or "morally correct" while judging others. We're torn within ourselves because we don't acknowledge or understand the two opposing sides within us, and our outer worlds reflect this inner chaos.

To unleash your whole best self, don't ignore your dark side; acknowledge that it exists and that it's OK—it just makes you human.

#2. Listen to what you find in your darkness

When you accept and sit to listen to your dark side, you'll find answers. You won't get there by pretending to be ideal. Asking yourself the truly difficult and uncomfortable questions can help you in many ways; it can show you the pain you've never healed from, the talent that you suppressed out of fear, or the dreams you didn't think you deserved to realize.

Be patient with yourself; this isn't easy work. You're literally choosing to confront your demons. You're doing it so that you can control them, instead of letting them control you. There may be several layers to uncover, but the more you do so, the more you'll see your whole true self and the more courageous you'll feel.

#3. Stop making yourself a victim

Life has its phases; it brings happiness and sorrow in waves. Some things will be in your control; others will not. But irrespective of how much control you have over external events, your internal world *is entirely in your hands.* You have complete power over your thoughts and emotions, even though you might feel helpless on your darkest days.

It's easy to feel like the victim when things haven't worked out despite your making your best attempts. But instead of resigning to your fate as a victim, try to learn from your negative experiences, thoughts, and emotions. Understand that no matter the past, only you are free to choose and shape your present and your future.

It might feel good temporarily to blame others; it helps you cope with loss, but it will *not* help you move forward. The key to reclaiming your power and control over life is to take sole responsibility and decide that you will shape your own future with your own choices.

#4. Learn how to shift perspective

As you learn how to listen to yourself more honestly and to unveil what both your wolves have to tell you, you'll get better at seeing things from different perspectives. You'll get better at both—looking at the world within you, and at the one outside you.

Maintain a journal—it's extremely helpful in articulating and observing patterns in your thoughts. Many people go through their entire lives without any introspection and without developing the maturity to understand that the same situation, person, or circumstance can be seen from different perspectives.

Many people go through their lives without listening to their inner voice and chasing their purest dreams. You're not going to be one of them.

#5. Stay calm, keep breathing, and ask for help

When you start to work with the darkness within you, it's possible that old memories and pains, especially ones you had buried, begin to surface.

Keep breathing; let your thoughts pass. Try to understand what the pain is trying to tell you. The more you let go of old and buried emotions, the freer you'll begin to feel. If you need to, reach out for help. You're committing to becoming the best version of yourself— don't leave any stone unturned. You will be terribly proud of yourself once you've made it into your future.

Chapter takeaways

- There's a light side and a dark side within each of us, and they're engaged in an eternal war. Which side you feed and strengthen is entirely up to you.

- It doesn't help to suppress and ignore your dark side; on the contrary, it can give you invaluable insights into yourself. You want to learn from it and wield it without letting it consume you.

- Stop victimizing yourself. Sit with your darkness and study what you find in it. It's your responsibility to bring yourself out of the darkness.

- Practice shifting perspective; seeing things from a different angle now and then can show you what you're missing out on or misunderstanding. To do your best in life and go all out in chasing your dreams, you need a calm and clear mind.

- Keep building a healthy and positive internal narrative, keep breathing, and keep asking for help when you need it. Keep feeding the right wolf.

"While one person hesitates because he feels inferior, the other is busy making mistakes and becoming superior."

— Henry C. Link

Crossing Over the Point of No Return
(and making a pivotal decision)

"When your self and your life belong to your being, your self opens, your life opens, your being comes in, and it will have everything. It is the single greatest turning point in your life."

John De Ruiter

Your life is shaped by your choices. It's shaped by the chances you take, as well as the ones you don't. It's a series of decisions at critical points that accumulate, pivoting your life down the path you find yourself on. These pivotal points span all areas of your life, from your education to your work and your relationships; they shape who you become.

When put together, they're what define you. You want to do your best then, at the time of making these crucial decisions. Only *you* are accountable. You may not always be ready to make them, you may not always feel equipped, and you may not always get the outcome you desire. And yet, making these decisions is the only way to move forward.

An important thing to understand about pivotal decision points is that they don't come too often—the lives of most people can be explained based on a few such key moments when they made a choice. One such example could be an artist deciding to relocate to Spain permanently. Another could be a couple deciding to file for a divorce. Or a CEO agreeing to a merger. Or an investment banker resigning to pursue her dream of becoming a chef.

Whether they're exhilarating or heartbreaking, pivotal moments set the course of your life. You don't need to constantly be very courageous, and you won't have to make life-altering decisions too frequently, but rather, you will need to summon up all your acumen, bravery, and clarity during a few periods in your life.

Try to reflect on the pivotal moments that have shaped your life. Perhaps you spent several years at law school while your friends were busy partying, and it has set you up for the rest of your life. Perhaps you never believed in marriage but went on a trip where you met the one person in the world who could convince you to believe otherwise, and you asked her to marry you. Or, you decided to drop out of college to save your parents from spending on tuition and built a thriving entrepreneurial venture.

Maybe you got a job you never imagined you'd get, and your family is relocating to an exotic foreign city as a result. Perhaps you've just gotten a loan approved to kick off your dream business.

You may find that you're extremely proud of some of your pivotal decisions. You may feel grateful for some others. And you may wonder about the rest. But you'll notice that all of these put you on the path to your own unique life journey.

Once you do make these, you'll find there is no going back. And if you're working from a place of clarity and determination as you've been learning to in this book, you won't want to or need to. The whole idea is to go after your dream life, with your *No Punches Pulled* approach by going all in, making pivotal decisions, and charging forward in relentless pursuit of your vision building towards your dreams.

You want to make choices from a place of confidence and determination, not from a place of pressure or helplessness. You want to make choices that reflect passion and hope, not fear. You want to push yourself to the point of no return. You want your commitment to be so complete that you don't care about going back.

Know that your pivotal decisions are what will differentiate your journey as an extraordinary one among a thousand others, and that only you can shape this journey.

Bracing for Pivotal Moments

Ask any successful person and they'll usually be able to point out just a handful of moments in their life that set in motion the series of events that would forever change everything. Do you know which moments these were for your life? What has brought you to your destiny? What important decisions are you putting off and why? What does your life look like five years from now? Have you decided how you're going to get there?

Don't worry if you haven't had a pivotal moment yet; you'll be prepared when it does present itself. You want to train your mind and your spirit to make the right decision with certainty, without doubt or fear.

Learning from pivotal moments in history

Here's some more information to inspire you and impress upon you the weight and responsibility of choosing correctly at crucial moments in time, not just for yourself, but for your family, community, company, or even country.

- Rosa Parks made history by refusing to give her seat on a bus in Alabama to a white passenger on board.

- Arnold Schwarzenegger began his career as a bodybuilder because he decided to enter a bodybuilding competition in Germany, having snuck out of the military barracks where he was in compulsory service.

- J. K. Rowling became one of the most successful authors ever by refusing to give up on her dream of a magical world no matter how many publishers rejected or ignored her.

- Viktor Frankl was liberated after spending years in concentration camps; he made the pivotal decision not to surrender his life or freedom, no matter the circumstances.

We all know the story of Bill Gates. We know the choices Steve Jobs made. We know about the decisions that shaped Barack Obama's life.

Your pivotal moments will come about once you realize exactly what meaning you want to give to your life. They will come about when you begin to take complete ownership, understanding that there was never any other way. And with these, you'll be on your way to crossing over to the point of no return.

Embracing challenges with open arms

An all-out approach to life will ask more courage of you than you're likely to see from anyone else around you. You have to believe in yourself and your dreams so thoroughly that you know you'll make them a reality.

The best challenges are a stretch. Double your income in ten years? Not so much of a challenge. Double your income next year? Now maybe that's a challenge. It might seem difficult to achieve, but it will only seem so if you stick to thinking the way you've always been thinking.

If you've just gotten a raise at work, you're unlikely to get your salary doubled a few months down the road. But if you've made up your mind and accepted the challenge, you'll figure out a way. Perhaps you'll launch a side hustle. Perhaps you'll pick up a night shift. You'll find a way to think out of the box, and sooner or later if not in exactly one year, you will double your income and meet your goal.

Whether you want to accept your challenges with passivity and resignation or with open arms and creative solutions is entirely up to you. Life is full of unforeseen challenges but is just as full of unexpected opportunities—that's what makes it so wonderful.

Train your mind to be ready and give yourself a winning shot. You can make anything possible.

Know that any destiny comes into being from action, from a constant flow of energy that pushes fears aside in favor of dreams. You want to retain your childlike belief in the magical and the extraordinary. You want to remind yourself how brave you once were. You want to ensure you become fearless again.

Your daily reminder: Carpe diem

When you truly belong to the present, when you are fully aware of your whole self in the here and now, and you are able to stay alive to the wonders of each fleeting day, your life will transform. If you are able to learn to be present to each and every moment, without half your mind switching around thinking about the past and the future, what you will experience in the unfolding of your life will be nothing short of magical.

The phrase "carpe diem," first used by Quintus Horatius, a Roman poet, translates to "pluck the day," or "harvest the day," or more appropriately translated, "seize the day." It is, in fact, part of a longer phrase that translates to 'seize the day and place little trust in tomorrow.'

In popular culture, this phrase has somehow come to mean "do whatever you want right now" or "YOLO" (you only live once). That's not what seizing the day is about. It's about grasping the true value of the present, about understanding it to be the gift that it is—because no one is promised a tomorrow.

You're reading this book because you want to maximize your chances of success, and you want to make it big in life. You want to learn how to make the best decisions at crucial moments on your journey. But in many ways, each day of your life and how you live it is a decision, isn't it? And these decisions compound.

The philosophy of carpe diem can be invaluable to you simply because it will impress upon you the importance of each day gone from your life. How did you decide to use the day? How much did you contribute? What difference did you make? How much did you truly seize the day—this one precious day, gone from the dream life you're building? You want to, on most days, be able to find happiness and pride in your answers to such questions.

5 Guidelines for Making a Pivotal Decision

How exactly can you train yourself to make better decisions at pivotal moments? How do you ensure you act from a place of clarity and strength, and not weight or confusion? Here are 5 key guidelines for you to practice.

#1 – Get comfortable being uncomfortable

If you're shaken up completely every time you're hit with an external trigger, or are easily upset, angered, or overwhelmed when things don't go your way, you need to train your mind to get comfortable in such situations. It may be developing greater self-awareness surrounding the circumstances that you need to make that pivotal life decision.

Learn to stay centered in the face of surprising bits of information or upon exposure to experiences outside of your comfort zone. I know this is easier said than done, which is why you need to build the capacity for this slowly over time. Accept and execute more actions that make you a little uncomfortable.

#2 – Learn how to meditate

Meditating regularly is a secret weapon of the most successful people in the world. Begin your day centering yourself and strengthening your mind; I can hardly think of a better way to start each new day.

#3 – Build your appetite for risk

Making good decisions requires confidence. And confidence comes from experience. It comes from knowing the results of certain choices, and from being able to assess risks sensibly and quickly.

To hone your decision-making ability, open up to making more and more decisions yourself, especially those that involve some degree of risk.

You might make mistakes—it's a part of the process. Learn how to forgive yourself for your mistakes, and refine your abilities to think and act more, from a place of greater wisdom.

#4 – Use social media to your advantage

If you're living in a silo or a bubble cut off from the world, it's harder to make the right difficult decisions when you're suddenly exposed to the realities around you. While the single most negative consequence of excessive social media usage is unhealthy comparison that keeps you distracted and insecure, it can also be used as a tool to stay on top of relevant affairs and developments in politics, across business, informed on interesting hobbies, and knowing more about the people you love.

#5 – Practice journaling daily

One of the best ways to get better at making decisions is very simple—track your decisions daily. If you're able to journal the thoughts and ideas that lead you to make your decisions, and capture obstacles that seem to hamper your decision-making skills, you can refer to your notes and gain valuable insights.

If you do this often enough and long enough, you should be able to see patterns: What risks scare you the most? What decisions were easy to make? Why did you struggle with the rest? Over time, equipped with this insight, you'll get better and more confident at making bigger decisions faster.

Chapter takeaways

- Though each individual's life is unique and comprises numerous choices, there are usually a handful of pivotal decisions taken at crucial moments that set their life path, for better or for worse.

- The idea is not to worry about such instances or reflect on decisions gone wrong, but to brace yourself for the future milestones in your life by learning to look at challenges in the face.

- Each day is a gift because tomorrow is never promised, and you want to be mindful because how you live and spend each day is what will compound. Carpe diem—seize the day today—don't live in the past, or in a future you can't yet see.

- To build your aptitude for making harder decisions faster at pivotal moments in your life, train for it. Put yourself in uncomfortable situations, build an appetite for risk and for the unknown to prevent overwhelm, meditate, use social media selectively and as a tool for growth, and practice journaling to build clarity.

Train to Win
(and join the 1% club)

"You must do today what nobody else will do, so tomorrow you can accomplish what others can't."

James Patterson

When you look around you, unless you find yourself doing what no one else is doing, you're likely to end up right where they end up. A critical component of success and a "No Punches Pulled" approach to life and work is a very simple one: **being determined**.

Your level of determination will either keep you operating at the same level as everyone else or set you apart. You must be able to push yourself to work harder, smarter, and longer than anyone else. That's what it takes to make it to the top. To be a part of the top 1% in any field of life, you've got to be willing to do what 99% of the rest won't.

The most successful people in any field did not reach the top by getting lucky, and don't listen to anyone who tells you so. They got there because they combined several strategies you've read about in this book, and consciously worked more than most of their peers could even imagine. They failed more than others, but always got back up, and in doing so, learned more than others. They understood that failure was not the opposite of success but, rather, an important part of it.

High-performance achievers were not born to win—they made it their business to win and trained harder than anyone else. They fed the right wolves inside them. They were obsessed with their goals. They didn't sit on their dreams—they did whatever it took, however long it took, to get where they wanted to be.

You want to be a part of this 1% club; otherwise, you wouldn't be reading this book. And in case you need to hear it—you've got what it takes to make it. But if you think you're getting there without training to win, and without outworking everyone else, or without pushing further than where everyone else stops pushing, you're mistaken.

There's no room for excuses in the 1% club

You might think you have very valid reasons for not being able to make it to the very top of your chosen field, or to have the very best life you can envision. Perhaps you were disadvantaged as a child in some form. Perhaps you grew up amid an abusive or unhealthy family environment.

Perhaps you were dyslexic, or you have ADHD. Perhaps you've had a failed marriage. Perhaps you were fired from a dream job, or unable to service your business debt and keep it afloat. Perhaps it's some other reason that you think is more unique and therefore justifies your not being on your way to the top. I'm here to tell you that no reason justifies it.

If you really want to succeed, no excuse is valid. And it's been proven to us, time and time again, by those who've actually made it.

We all know what a legend **Oprah** is. She's got one of the most famous success stories in the world and inspires millions of people across geographies and generations. What you may not know is that she was born desperately poor, grew up living on welfare, and was raised by a single mother, deeply abused as a child, pregnant as a teenager with a baby that was lost, and struggled well into young adulthood. She then turned her life around and didn't stop until she became the brilliant mogul she is today.

Another no-excuses rags-to-riches story is that of **Jay-Z**. He grew up selling drugs. He grew up doing whatever he had to get by in Brooklyn. He embraced his humble beginnings and worked extraordinarily hard to level up. He began by selling music CDs out of his car, started his own label, then built an album with which he rose to fame, and worked day and night ever since to stay at the top.

Henry Ford, the father of the modern age, made mistake after mistake, learning from one failure after another. Before he championed the assembly line and became the famous creator of the automobile, he built two companies that went bankrupt.

Do you know how much work went into Mickey Mouse being born? Though you might find it hard to imagine, **Walt Disney** was fired from his first job for not being creative enough. He went on to build an empire based on the most creative cartoons (and as it turns out, subsequently bought the company he had been fired from).

Van Gogh was a paranoid schizophrenic and was able to sell only one painting during his lifetime, and even that was only to a close friend.

Actor **Chris Pratt** took twenty years to go from being paid $700 for his first movie to being paid $10 million to film the thrilling blockbuster success *Jurassic World.*

Lastly, even though today he features as one of the top three to four richest men on earth, **Bill Gates** has had a story with more failures and setbacks than the average person can comprehend. His was a journey of product malfunctions and market failures much before it was the success story of Microsoft.

Anytime you find yourself slacking or feeling lost—think about these personalities and their stories and let them fuel you to not give up.

Understanding and Exercising Willpower

It's possible that you don't really know how willpower operates. It sounds like a vague term; it seems to us something that we're either born with or not. It seems that some people just have a lot of it somehow. It isn't so. A more appropriate explanation of determination, or willpower if you want to call it that, is that it acts like a muscle; it can be exercised, exhausted, and strengthened by training.

In an attempt to explain willpower through the lens of science, author Kelly McGonigal in her book *The Willpower Instinct*, states that research tells us willpower comes from, not only the brain but, also the body. In order to do what you know is right, as opposed to giving in to your bodily urges and cravings such as smoking or overeating, you need to strengthen your prefrontal cortex, or the part of your brain that is responsible for helping in decision-making and behavior control.

The way to strengthen this, just as is the case with other muscles, is to give it the necessary fuel or food and time for recovery with sleep.

McGonigal also suggests that much like other muscles do when they're continuously exercised, willpower gets "exhausted," so you want to be careful in how you deplete it. You want to reduce its use for fighting distractions and controlling your anger, and exercise it instead for creativity, productivity, and joy.

Your 10-Point Guide to Rethinking Failure

Whether in a personal capacity or in a professional one, you can't become tremendously successful without facing any failure. You don't want to run from failure—on the contrary, you want to fail more so that you can learn more, and you want to fail big so that you can succeed massively. You just want to make sure you're failing smart, and not repeating your mistakes.

Here's a quick 10-point guide that will show you how to completely change your mindset with regard to how you view failure, so that you can win big.

1 – Failures are only stepping stones

When you fail, how do you typically react? Do you feel ashamed? Embarrassed? Humiliated? Insecure? Angry?

Conversely, how do you feel when you succeed? Happy? Proud? Popular? I want you to take a step back for a moment and think of your reactions to failure and success, and to study why you feel the way you do.

How much did you truly learn from your successes? And comparatively, how much did you learn every time you failed? I'm certain you learned a great deal more from your failures, provided you actively reflected on them.

What you do wrong can be much more valuable than what you do right in the long run, simply because it teaches you right from wrong and leaves you wiser, stronger, and better equipped for bigger opportunities down the road. You may have heard the saying, "The one who falls and gets back up is much stronger than the one who never fell."

Falling and getting back up is hard. Everyone faces setbacks—no exceptions. But many never recover. Those who do, those who know that this is indeed the road to success, win big. So, don't expect a red carpet to success—you won't find one.

Decide today that your obstacles are only trying to teach you something new. Expect failures in the shape of stepping stones, and you'll be well on your way to success.

2 – Failure is largely driven by fear

In most cases, people don't succeed because they're so afraid to fail that they never even try. It's fear that is killing their dreams, and causing them to fail, rather than any other obstacles on the path. If you're letting your fear stop you, or are too afraid to take risks, you're certainly not going to succeed.

You can fail countless times. You can make a thousand mistakes. You can fall and get back up over and over. But you can't be afraid. There's no room for fear in the 1% club.

3 – Bigger failures can fuel greater successes

We have a tendency to take small steps and play small so that even if we lose, we don't lose much. And naturally, this keeps us from gaining much as well. In Kennedy's words, "Only those who dare to fail greatly can ever achieve greatly."

The bigger your dream, the bigger your attempts will be, and by extension, you will have bigger failures, and more frequent ones. If you don't have a predecessor to learn from or are working on an innovation with no precedents, naturally, there isn't much for you to directly learn from. You'll have to try new things—sometimes you'll fail. And then, you'll succeed, in a way no one ever has before.

4 – Failure forces innovation, creativity, and bravery

Do you remember what Edison said about all his failures before he got his invention right? He said he hadn't failed, but rather discovered a thousand different ways of why something would not work.

Each failure pushes for a different solution. Each failure demands more creativity and courage. Multiple failures are not for the faint-hearted, and staying the course rewards the brave multifold.

5 – Failure is often about timing

In some cases, creations are considered failures because they're ahead of their time or don't belong to the society they have been envisioned within. Think of any of the most famous artists in the world. Van Gogh was thought a madman by his peers. Most of Michelangelo's work, including the legendary *David*, would have struggled to find acceptance during his time had it not been for the patronage of the Medici family. It took centuries for such work and their creators to find the appreciation they deserved, and these men were anything but failures.

Even outside of the realm of art, a great business idea might fail if it is positioned to the wrong audience, or under the wrong circumstances. Failure isn't anything other than a need to revisit your product, service, or art from a more holistic perspective, to learn where you're going wrong, and then to try once more, at a different time.

6 – Understanding failure helps you understand success

It's said you can only appreciate the light because you've seen the darkness. Similarly, you may have an entirely different perspective of success if you come to it after having known failure.

Failing is important because it helps you see better. It helps you refine your skills and yourself, showing you what you would have never otherwise discovered, bringing you to heights you would never else have managed to climb to, or remain at, if you hadn't learned from the hardships on your journey.

If you find yourself in tough spots and hard times, you want to be grateful for the lessons that these will inevitably bring—they're preparing you for your destiny.

7 – Failures show you how to shape what defines you and what doesn't

Only you can decide what defines you. If you want to let your mistakes and your failure define you—that's up to you. If you want to make a massive comeback that will define you instead—that's entirely up to you as well.

Just know that you can't blame others. Only you get to decide and are responsible for deciding what shapes you.

8 – Failures show you how to love your mistakes

Somewhere down the road, most of us have picked up the idea that it's not OK to make mistakes. In general, mistakes are not encouraged—not by our teachers at school, not by our parents as we grow up, and not by our managers at work. And yet, making mistakes and failing is the best way to learn.

Now that you understand this discrepancy, it's up to you to change your mindset when it comes to making mistakes. Go on—make many mistakes. They're only wrong under one condition—when you learn nothing from them.

9 – Failing teaches you self-love

Many people go through life being kind, patient, and graceful with others, but not so with themselves. How kind are you to yourself? Are you aware of how much your internal narrative affects your mind and spirit?

Do you speak to yourself kindly, or are you always critical and toxic in your own thoughts about yourself, whether it's with regard to your self-image, education, relationships, or work? How do you treat yourself when you fail?

Self-talk is much more important than you give it credit. The most successful people in the world are also their own biggest cheerleaders, irrespective of what anyone around them is thinking or saying.

Let's say you fail. Don't let yourself feel angry. Don't let yourself feel inadequate. Don't beat yourself up. So what if you failed today? You won't tomorrow.

Be kind to yourself, encourage yourself, and positively critique yourself, just as you do for a loved one around you.

10 – Failing fuels determination and consistency of action

Perhaps the biggest advantage of failing is that it motivates you to take massive, consistent action as well as few other things can. When the goal truly matters, failure will only create more resolve to reach it. You'll know your previous action was wrong or wasn't good enough. You'll rectify your mistakes, you'll course correct, you'll get back on track, you'll keep at it, and with this, you'll get whatever it is you want.

In most cases, it's consistency of effort that creates success; it's what you do every day, even on the hardest days, that brings you to the top 1%, not what you do once in a while influenced by a burst of motivation.

The same applies to leading a company—it's years and years of gradual growth and sustained profits that build giants, with failures overcome and crises dealt with in the journey. As a leader, keep in mind the words of Andy Grove: "Bad companies are destroyed by crises; good companies survive them; great companies are improved by them."

To learn more about learning from failure and leveraging it for maximum success, refer to my book *Fail Big*. **Fail big** and fail often; just don't stop until you win.

Your NPP Ticket to the Top 1%

You know by now that failure precedes success. Once you've mastered the art of overcoming and learning from failure, you have a powerful foundation. You have your launchpad—it's now time to chase massive success.

Here's your 10-step ticket to train to win. You'll learn how to outwork everyone else. You'll learn how to get to the top 1%. You'll build the determination to do what others will never attempt. And you'll get further than they'll ever dream of.

#1 – Define your own version of success

Before you can accelerate down the road to any goals, you want to ensure the goals you're chasing are aligned with what success means to you. What others set as their goals are not your goals. What others expect of you is also not what should define your success. It's your version and definition of success that matters.

Let others buy new cars. Let them buy bigger homes. Let them travel first class. If that's what you want—go ahead and plug it into your vision road map. But if it isn't, it's perfectly alright. Your version of success could be something very different, for instance, helping others or saving the planet.

You've got to decide and define what success means to you—that's step 1 in getting to the 1%, and in training to win.

#2 – Take complete ownership

Decide today—no matter how hard things get, no more complaining or whining. You are entirely in control of your journey. Even if you're hit with external, unforeseen circumstances that turn things upside down, it's only you that must control your response.

In the 1% club, you'll only meet people who are in complete control—there's no place for blame games and playing the victim. Taking *complete ownership* and being fully invested in your own purpose also means you have no time to compare and criticize others. Quit talking about all the things that are unfair and why others don't deserve their successes—and instead focus on your own journey.

You might turn around and say luck plays a part—perhaps it does. But even for luck to help you, fortune to favor you, or for the tide to turn, you've got to be in the right place, at the right time, fully prepared.

Don't sit around waiting for luck. Work hard and then work harder; if and when luck does strike, it will only act as an amplifier to your efforts toward success.

#3 – Decide to let go of things you cannot control

No individual on earth can control everything. That's not to say what's outside of your control isn't hard for you to deal with, whether it's a political situation, the repercussions of a law, or a family member's decisions.

You can certainly help others and contribute toward causes you care about, but this is different from understanding that you can't control the outcome of everything, and that all outcomes are not black and white or instant.

Remember, you cannot change others—they will only change if and when they want to change. The only thing you have complete control over is yourself—so why not focus on improving yourself?

#4 – Learn to ask for feedback

Each individual has strengths. And though it might not seem very obvious, each individual also has weaknesses. Including the members of the 1% club. The difference is, most people hide their weaknesses, lie to themselves about them, or ignore them. The people in the 1% club don't; they accept them, improve on them, and ask for help and feedback.

You will need help from time to time, whether it's in terms of resources, knowledge, moral support, or love. Reach out to the people you trust—the ones who know both your strengths and weaknesses, and will be honest, critical as well as encouraging.

#5 – Stop beating yourself up with competition

I want you to repeat this to yourself as many times as it takes for you to truly believe it: Your only real competition is your former self. Not anyone around. You won't get to the 1% club if you're putting all your time and energy in staying on top of others' Instagram accounts. You will get to the 1% club by focusing on yourself and improving on who you were yesterday.

This is not to say competition with others is not healthy—it can be an excellent way for both you and your competitor to push and bring out your best selves. Many people respect their most cutthroat competitors, as well as celebrate each other's successes. Many competitors are also the best of friends; they understand that another's win is not necessarily their loss in the larger scheme of things.

If your competition is making you better, great! But if you're using it to beat yourself up, you're going about it wrong and you're better off focusing on yourself. Envy and jealousy can be the toughest of human emotions to deal with and can drain you of all of your energy for a long time if you let them.

Bitterness and resentment are hard to hold in your heart. If you find yourself feeling these, remember that someone else's success doesn't equal your failure—the world is big enough, abundant enough and magical enough for everyone's dreams to come true—life is not a zero-sum game.

#6 – Play long-term games

You might feel like you are way behind your peers. Perhaps they're earning millions of dollars and you aren't.

Perhaps they have children, and you don't. Perhaps they're very fit, and you're not. At times it might feel hard to believe, but life is not a race. There are no set timelines. Everyone's journey is beautifully unique, and to compare it to another, to push it so that it unfolds within the boundaries of some norms, takes away from its potential, fullness, and magic.

The best way to snap out of short-term thinking is to ask yourself, Will this matter in five years? Will it matter in fifty? You'll probably find that if it does matter, you will find a way to resolve it with time. So, don't worry about it and stick to your path with all your faith and determination.

#7 – Stay focused – don't fall for the instant gratification trap

If you give in to every impulse, it's hard to get ahead. If you buy everything you're advertised, it's hard to save. If you go out for a party every time you're invited, it's hard to stay on top of schoolwork.

Learning to resist instant gratification for long-term gain is crucial to success. Know that you'll only see results once you've put in time, effort, and commitment, and focusing means saying "no" when you need to.

#8 – Count your blessings, even on your hardest days

The first thing in the morning or the last thing before you fall asleep must be a quick practice of gratitude. It will only take you a couple of minutes to count your blessings each day, but over time, you'll find yourself wired to look at your life very differently. You'll see things from a positive perspective—you'll see the good amid the bad, and as you want the good to amplify, why not focus on it and be grateful for it?

#9 – Don't run from pain

You may have seen a popular quote from Muhammad Ali doing the rounds on the Internet that says that he only starts counting his sit-ups when they start to hurt, because the ones before those aren't the ones that count. Pain is OK, as long as it aligns with your purpose and your goal.

It's not about showing others how much you can endure; it's about building your own capacity, emotionally, mentally, and physically. To win big, don't run from hardship or pain. Let it come—you'll face it. You'll learn from it. You'll become better and better, until you're the best.

#10 – Be both, realistic and optimistic

To get to the 1%, you will certainly need to be optimistic, and I'm sure you are. But you need to balance your optimism with reality, so that you aren't operating in a bubble. Living in a dream world does not help unless those dreams fuel action in the present, and that comes from being aligned with reality.

You don't want to be overwhelmed by your current circumstances; it doesn't matter where you are today—it only matters where you want to go. But it's important to know where you are today, so that you can begin your journey to your dreams, and it's one grounded in reality.

Chapter takeaways

- To get to the top 1% of any area in life, you need to be more determined than others, and you need to be willing to do what others won't. If nothing separates you from them, and you aren't doing anything that they aren't, you're likely to end up where they will.

- In your journey to success, take complete ownership, leave no room for excuses, and welcome luck if and when it comes, but don't depend on it or wait for it.

- Don't believe that you either have strong willpower or not—understand that it functions like a muscle that can be strengthened.

- Take the time to entirely rethink your perspective of failure. Failure can be a better teacher than anyone on earth. Failure is often about fear and timing, forces creativity and courage, helps you understand success better, helps you shape yourself better, and fuels consistent action.

- To get to the 1% club, begin by defining your version of success. Focus on long-term plays, let go of things outside your control, forget about instant gratification, and embrace pain.

The Power of Hyper-focus
(and Living by Your Optimal Schedule)

"The key is in not spending time, but in investing it."

Stephen R. Covey

We take time for granted. We hear things like "time is of the essence" and dismiss them. We think ten minutes here or thirty minutes there doesn't really matter. We forget that the minutes add up to make the hours, which make the days, which make the years. This chapter is going to reinforce the essence of time, the need to focus and stick to your optimal schedule, and to build momentum in your "No Punches Pulled" approach to life.

It's time to get rid of all the irrelevant and pointless time-wasting activities you engage in. It's time to set limits to your television and Netflix bingeing, to put the break on hours spent scrolling down social media feeds, and to put an end to all other ways of killing time.

It's worthwhile to remember that it isn't setting a schedule that matters—most people do that. Almost everyone I know makes a to-do list every day. The problem is, we think in terms of days, not hours or minutes. If we were to look at a day in terms of 15-minute slots and see how many of these we actually utilized productively and how many we wasted, we'd think about time very differently. We'd execute things better. And at the end, it's the **execution in alignment with a strategy** that delivers the punch with impact.

Rapid Action and the Power of Momentum

You could be a master planner. You could be the most promising strategist. You could have a world-changing idea. But without action, all of this is meaningless.

It is focus and action, when put together, that smashes boundaries and puts you well on your way to success and happiness. It is only when you make up your mind to snap out of your lethargy, stop procrastinating, and somehow get yourself to begin to do all of the things on your schedule that results start to emerge.

It is important to take intentional action, and to take it quickly. It is important to build momentum with a rigor that few will match. It is important to do what others won't. It is important to spend your time well. It is important to understand how limited time is, and how soon it passes by, whether it's used efficiently or not.

You might remember Jack Kornfield's words: "The trouble is, you think you have time." You don't—none of us do. And if we were to truly understand the gravity of this, we would quit wasting a single moment. We would stop fooling around with our deadlines. We would quit looking for the next distraction that steals focus and robs us of time.

If you knew something could be accomplished in one day, you wouldn't ask for a month to do it. You would stop drifting about, hoping to reach your goals someday. You would move faster, so that you could beat others moving slower and taking it easier than you. You would do whatever it takes to take intentional action and execute your plans, without excuses, as fast as you could. You would truly be all in.

The Power of 17 Seconds

I want to show you a technique that will impress upon you the power of time, and the results of using it well. It's called the 17-second rule. That's all—just 17 seconds, and you're on your way to magic.

Adapted from the Law of Attraction, the rule states that *simply visualizing what you want and feeling the sense of accomplishment that will come with achieving your goal for as little as 17 seconds is powerful enough to train your mind to focus better toward the goal.*

Even if you don't believe in the Law of Attraction, think of this as a simple technique to help you make a conscious mental shift, taking you from wherever you are into the state you want to be in, creating a stronger pull toward your goal.

There is enough evidence to support that at least 50% of our brains are malleable—the thoughts we reinforce and encourage are embedded deeper and deeper within us. We can choose to focus on the bad or to dwell on what's amiss. Or, we can choose to boost our brains with thoughts of what we want, and fill ourselves with emotions of love, accomplishment, success, and abundance.

It's just as easy (or difficult) to wire your brain for the good as it is for the bad. It's entirely up to you—you and only you can choose your recurring thoughts. And you have the power to shape this beginning with mindset and mood shifts that take as little as 17 seconds.

That's 17 seconds of holding one thought consistently, by visualizing or reaffirming your goals, without allowing negative thoughts to interrupt, completely changes the frequency or energy at which you're operating.

You can go from angry to calm, or from sad to peaceful. If you're able to hold the thought for longer, you increase the strength of this thought; you give it more power over you. It starts to reside within you.

The thought that began with 17 seconds builds its own momentum and attracts other similar thoughts to it. The more you hold on to, and act from, vibrations of compassion, love, empathy, joy and abundance, the higher the chances of motivated and focused action, and the higher your chances of all your desires manifesting.

The 5-step NPP Hyper-focus Checklist

Here are five key steps to build hyper-focus so that you can stick to your optimal schedule. It's time to boost your energy and speed in getting things done by taking rapid action *now*. It's time to build that momentum toward your goals.

#1 – Think of your day in terms of 15-minute slots

The first step to living in focus and adherence with your optimal schedule is to shake up how you think of your day. You don't have a "full workday" of eight hours ahead of you; you have thirty-two slots of 15 minutes each. To extract the most of your day, then, you want to make the most of these slots. I'm not saying this means taking no breaks; by all means, schedule two slots for yoga and one slot for a coffee.

I'm saying whatever you want to slot into your day has to be a conscious decision. If you want to spend four slots watching Netflix and two slots on Instagram—that's up to you. But for the rest of your slots, you want to then stay fixated on the work in front of you, with no distractions.

#2 – Track what you're working on

You might say that since you've made a schedule, this step is redundant, but it isn't. To become tremendously successful, you need to watch your time like a hawk. You don't have a single minute to spare—unless you decide to. Setting a schedule is easy; reflecting on how well you stuck to it and assessing how you *really* spend your time is harder, but this is what will help you eventually align with your optimal schedule.

#3 – Set reasonable agendas – stick to 2–3 important tasks each day

Which are the three tasks you absolutely must focus on today? Write them down and make sure you complete them. These could be the toughest ones, the ones that you are most hesitant to get done—but make sure you get them done. Don't overschedule your day and burn yourself out. Start each day in attack mode, and you'll stay on top of your days.

#4 – Prioritize around importance and urgency

It's natural to want to "get things off your plate." Got an email—why not respond to it right away and be done with it? Twitter is ablaze—why not add a quick tweet? You might be used to responding "quickly"—but this is very different from responding to what *needs* your time and energy. How important is it, truly, to respond to that email right away? Or to write that tweet right away? It probably isn't.

Out of all the things you think you need to do, many things might simply not be required at all. You may be putting out fires all day, only to realize at the end of the day that you never got around to any important work. I want you to think about how to categorize your work tasks in terms of "importance" and "urgency."

You might have heard of the Eisenhower Matrix; it's a well-known time management tool. It suggests that you categorize your tasks into four types, and execute them in the following order of priority:

Type 1: Tasks that are both urgent and important

Type 2: Tasks that are important but not urgent (these are the tasks you do yourself)

Type 3: Tasks that are urgent but unimportant (these are the tasks you delegate)

Type 4: Tasks that are neither urgent nor important (these are the tasks you delete from your to-do list)

As you can see, it isn't just about doing things quickly; it's about what things you are doing, and in what order of priority. Developing the ability to focus on what's truly worth your while is integral to success.

#5 – Protect your time from the nonessential

In the typical office environment, there's a lot we've gotten used to and accepted as "normal." For instance, we're used to one-hour-long meetings, even when the same agenda can be covered in forty minutes.

We're used to being interrupted because of open-floor plans. We're used to "group discussions" that may or may not extract the brightest ideas from us. We're used to switching from one task to the next and struggling to get back to complete what we originally set out to do. We're used to repetitive, administrative work that can and should be automated, simply because we've always done it, and others have always done it. What this also means is that, we're used to wasting time.

This isn't you, at least not anymore. This isn't how you want to work. You're committed to achieving the maximum, in the minimum amount of time, freeing up more time to do more work.

So, begin to passionately get rid of the nonessential time-sucking activities and tasks you may have gotten used to doing. Write everything down—what tasks you undertook, how long they took, how many breaks you needed, how many distractions you faced, how many people interrupted you—get as granular as you can.

When you study this from a distance, and see where you're spending time, you might have surprising insights. Once you've clearly identified problems, you can begin to design solutions. You're likely to realize you can get *much* more work done, in *much* less time, if you just *focus*.

Chapter takeaways

- You cannot have a "No Punches Pulled" approach to life without understanding the importance of time. Remember that the minutes add up to make the hours, which make the days, which make the months and the years. Time does not wait.

- The best planning, the most innovative ideas and the best laid out strategies are pointless without action. You need to take the first actionable step, and you need to take it now, and once you have, you need to build momentum to keep going.

- It takes as little as 17 seconds of holding on to a thought with focus and clarity to induce a mindset and mood shift. Practice holding a thought consistently, by visualizing or affirming your goals, for just 17 seconds at a time, and begin to see how your energy, vibration, and frequency shifts.

- To boost your energy for getting things done and to build hyper-focus to stick to your optimal schedule, begin by changing how you think of your day—think in terms of 15-minute slots.

- Track what you're working on and set fewer tasks for your day but make sure you complete them. Learn how to get better at prioritizing around importance and urgency, and at protecting your time from nonessential activities.

Train Your Mind to Crave Discomfort
(and push beyond your comfort zone)

"I think goals should never be easy, they should force you to work, even if they are uncomfortable at the time."

Michael Phelps

There is no road to success that does not involve growth, and growth comes from pushing past boundaries. It comes from being able to do what you once couldn't. It comes from embracing change, from stepping out of your comfort zone. The more you're able to be comfortable with being uncomfortable, the better primed you are to grow.

What you want lies outside of your comfort zone—that's where a world of opportunities awaits, if you're able to and ready to reach out. Everything that you've ever wanted is on the other side of your fear, and to get there requires you to do whatever it takes.

This chapter is about getting yourself ready to get uncomfortable, and to train your mind to first accept this state of growth, and then to master it. You're first going to learn how to get comfortable with discomfort, and then how to thrive in it. You don't have to expect being comfortable doing things you've never done overnight;

you only have to get started in building the capacity to do so.

Take small strides if you must, but take them, in the right direction, and you'll find growth.

Why we avoid being uncomfortable

We're hardwired to stay within the realm of what we know and understand. In choosing between the comfort of doing the same thing we have always done, and the pain of doing something we don't like even though it might lead to something better, we tend to choose the former. Stepping out of our comfort zone doesn't come easily or naturally to us—it requires courage and discipline, and sometimes outright boldness.

When people are faced with uncomfortable situations when they aren't ready for them or equipped to take on them, they're stressed. They might turn to smoking, doing hard drugs, drinking excessively, shopping excessively, or overworking crazy hours to numb the pain.

All these are methods of denial and ways to stay away from the discomfort of the thing that's staring them in the eye. But as I'm sure you're aware, no good comes of this. The base emotion driving such behavior is fear—a fear of change, of growth, of being uncomfortable. Admitting this fear is the first step to acquiring familiarity and comfort with change—and that's the only way forward.

Avoiding being uncomfortable cannot help you grow, no matter what you might have come to believe. If you've been sedentary for too long and you begin to exercise, you will feel discomfort. If you've been eating junk food for years and you change your diet, you will feel discomfort. Any time you're doing something you're not used to doing or have perhaps never done, there will be discomfort. And that's a part of growth. In fact, doing hard things even when they hurt is the foundation on which growth is built.

You want to remind yourself that being uncomfortable isn't a bad thing—it just means you're doing something you're not used to. It is the price you pay for growth and success. If you're willing to pay the price, anything is possible.

The NPP Discomfort Challenge – Stage 1: Acceptance

Here are eight ways to get yourself into the practice of discomfort. The more you accept that you're OK being uncomfortable, the more you can gradually learn to push your horizons.

#1 – Do one more rep

To begin, it's as simple as this—whatever you are used to doing, do just a little bit more. One more push-up. One more page of writing. One more meeting before you call it a day. Don't underestimate the potential of small steps toward progress.

#2 – Take a hard look at your fears

I promise you, a lot of what's keeping you stuck in your comfort zone is just fear. Are you afraid of what others might think or say? Are you afraid of messing up your first shot at something new? Are you afraid you'll make a fool of yourself? Take a hard look at what's keeping you from pushing further.

#3 – Embrace your thoughts

Don't run from your own thoughts. Spend time practicing mindfulness each day. You don't have to believe every thought you think or every emotion you feel—learn to let these thoughts pass through. You're prepping your mind for the courage to do new things— you'll need it to be calm.

#4 – Get your essentials in order

All said and done, it's harder to push yourself to newer opportunities and challenges if you don't have your basics in order. Get real about your debt—and create a plan of action to get on top of it. Get real about your health issues and find a way to address them. Without the basics in place, you can't build sustainable momentum.

#5 – Get organized

This means getting rid of the clutter in your physical space as well as on digital media. A simple change in how your work desk looks, how neatly your clothes are organized, or how well categorized all your apps are on your phone can get the ball rolling toward positive change.

#6 – Build clarity with regard to your mission

Knowing your purpose, what you want and why exactly you want it is an integral part of being able to accept whatever comes your way in your pursuit. So, take the time to do whatever you need to build that clarity of purpose.

#7 – Have a long-term plan to embrace discomfort, but start taking small steps today

Don't expect to be jumping out of your comfort zone tomorrow; let this take its time. Just focus on taking small steps every day.

Stop procrastinating. Try that new salad. Or that new workout. Make a new friend. Take a new class.

In the words of Eleanor Roosevelt: "Do one thing every day that scares you. Those small things that make us uncomfortable help us build courage to do the work we do."

#8 – Be willing to pay the price for success

As mentioned previously, American oil tycoon H. L. Hunt said: "First, decide exactly what it is you want. Most people never do that. Second, determine the price you're going to have to pay to get it, and then resolve to pay that price."

All achievement has a price to pay. If you want to participate in the Olympics, be prepared to train hard even on your off days to master the sport you want to compete in. To build your own business, working a regular nine-to-five job won't cut it, as you'll need to work when you can, as much as you can to make it successful. If you want to lose weight, giving up on comfort food is the price you must pay.

Whatever the price is, rest assured that someone out there is willing to pay it to make it. You must be, too.

This means getting really uncomfortable with pushing past old behaviors and the comfort of established boundaries.

What is the price you must pay, and how do you resolve to pay it?

The NPP Discomfort Challenge – Stage 2: Mastery

Now that you're getting more comfortable with being uncomfortable, and your mind is more accepting of change and growth, it's time to build some momentum. Here are the next seven steps on your journey to mastering discomfort.

#1 – Go looking for challenges instead of waiting for them to appear

To those obsessed with success, waiting is not an option. It's time to go after what you want, instead of hoping for good luck to bring fortune. The NPP framework is about taking direct action and chasing your dreams down relentlessly—so begin chasing those challenges.

#2 – Let your small steps toward discomfort snowball

You've been adding a little something new to your workouts for the past three months, and are excited to sign up for that intensive Tabata class? Go for it, now! You're getting the hang of accepting and enjoying new things.

#3 – Do what you've never done before

What have you always been afraid to try? Find a way to go do it. And once you have, pick another fear to face.

Train your mind to know—the best things are not the easiest to pursue, at least not at first.

#4 – Listen to, and understand, what your discomfort is telling you

You've begun to push your boundaries—great. You want to assess how you feel as you get a bit uncomfortable. What is your first response to doing something new? Do you immediately try to find an excuse? Are you really opening up to embracing change?

#5 – Smile through the pain of the new

Don't dismiss this advice—yes, you certainly want to build comfort with growth, but you want to enjoy this journey. If you can truly learn to be *happy* with discomfort, your growth will know no bounds. Keep smiling through all your discomfort—you're growing, not struggling.

#6 – Build a support system

Support from like-minded well-wishers can be invaluable in your pursuit of the mastery of growth. Make sure you have your cheerleaders, your advisors, your constructive critics—talk to them about your fears and experiences.

#7 – Celebrate your progress and improve with repetition

As you grow step by step, and then by leaps and bounds, track your progress. It always helps to understand your own patterns, so that you can apply them better when you next need to. You're going to be able to feel the change—track this accomplishment in real time and celebrate it.

Lastly, remember that repetition solidifies what you learn. Whatever your new activity might be, rinse, and repeat, until you can't get it wrong. See what it does for your growth and confidence.

Chapter takeaways

- Accept that there can be no success without growth, and no growth without pushing boundaries. Unless you embrace change and step out of your comfort zone, you won't grow.

- Admitting your fear of something is the first step to acquiring a sense of comfort with change, and it's the only way forward.

- Begin with small steps to get OK being uncomfortable, and gradually learn to push your horizons more and more. Get organized, get your essentials and finances in order. Practice mindfulness and listen to your fears.

- Be clear about where you want to get to; clarity will fuel your growth. And try to do one new thing every day, no matter how small or simple it might seem— you're building your own capacity to do more and more things that scare you.

- Once you've tasted discomfort and are acquainted with it, it's time to step on the gas. Go looking for challenges– don't wait for them to present themselves. Attempt big and new things now—do what you've never done. Build your support system.

- Celebrate your small wins and repeat your practices. And remember to smile through it all and enjoy your journey of growth.

"*Like success, failure is many things to many people. With Positive Mental Attitude, failure is a learning experience, a rung on the ladder, a plateau at which to get your thoughts in order and prepare to try again.*"

— W. Clement Stone

Take Control of Your Day
(and Build Intention into Your Purpose)

"No one saves us but ourselves. No one can and no one may.

We ourselves must walk the path."

Buddha

Our lives are made up of our years; our years are made up of our days. Having one bad day can feel pretty harmless. They grow into a couple of bad days and you've had a bad week; you don't think it's much of a problem. But before you know it, it's been a bad month—and you begin to see that you're falling behind and have to play catch-up.

No one sees only good days all throughout their lives; good and bad are two sides of the same coin. It is essential then for us to learn how to keep going even on our bad days and how to make the most of them. And when the good days come, we can be grateful for the smooth sailing.

The ability to take control of each day, especially the bad days, and the skill to stay on top of your goals for the day rather than letting the day overwhelm you is a common trait of those who win at life and succeed in everything they do. Controlling the day implies that you control yourself, your emotions, your energy, your focus and your time.

You're neither a puppet to external circumstances nor a prey of runaway emotions and thoughts, but rather, the captain of your own ship. You dictate how you will shape the day, one after the other, and in doing so, shape your life experience.

There is a reason why CEOs begin the day with meditation and why athletes train their mind and body first thing in the morning. The idea is to get a head start, to begin each new day or opportunity on the offense rather than defense. High performers like to take control of their energy, emotions, and thoughts as soon as they're awake, and know that winning the morning implies winning the day.

When you wake up early, deeply rested, and start the day with a clear head and a focused approach to tackle the day ahead, you've won half the battle. A powerful morning routine helps the most successful people in the world use each day to the fullest, driving them toward becoming limitless in life. Whereas several others will have begun their mornings stressing, reminiscing about past regrets, worrying about the future, or being overwhelmed by their ongoing problems.

Beginning the day with a healthy morning routine lowers your chances of losing control of the day. When you're in control of your internal environment—thoughts and emotions—you're less likely to allow external forces to dictate your time and space. You're less likely to be distracted. You live with intention and aggression, as opposed to going about your day passively, apathetically, or on autopilot.

Lastly, you're much more likely to be calm, because you've premeditated on the various options and outcomes, and addressed the chaos in your mind.

Remember, taking control of the day is not just about getting more done each day (though that might certainly be an effect). It's just as much about doing the things that matter, and about making conscious use of your time and effort.

You're reading this book because you are on a mission to build a "No Punches Pulled" approach to managing your life and your time. Taking control of your days, and of the moments that make up your days by making intentional decisions to take deliberate action, is the way to begin.

Urgency is powerful, and too much patience can hold you back

We've grown up learning that "Good things come to those who wait." We've grown up being told "Be patient and your time will come." We've come to believe "We're just paying our dues." We grow up believing that patience is a virtue, and it is. But alongside this, we forget to remember that there is a very high cost associated with not acting with urgency when situations demand it. Certain opportunities require an urgent response or will pass by. Another mistake far too many people make is confusing patience with inaction or procrastination.

Waiting for something without taking actionable steps toward it isn't patience; waiting for something while doing absolutely everything that is in your control, with faith in the ultimate outcome, no matter how hard the journey, is the path forward that leads to sustainable progress.

We hear countless stories of people who spend their lives waiting. They're stuck for decades in unfulfilling jobs, waiting for the perfect day to change their lives. They wait for the perfect business idea to strike. They wait to have enough money to travel. They wait for their relationships to get better without taking ownership. They wait to retire to paint, or write, or build their dream home. They wait for the economy to get better. They wait for favorable laws to be passed. They wait for their spouses or employers to be in a better mood. They wait for luck to find them. They wait for fortune to smile upon them.

They wait and wait, believing that their patience will be rewarded someday. And sometimes it is, but more often than not, it is not. Because while they were waiting, someone out there was already making things happen.

Someone else with the same dream, perhaps with fewer resources, but with more determination, was taking control of their days, months, years, and doing whatever it took to make their dreams come true, beginning right there and then, not waiting for later.

Don't get me wrong—patience is necessary. But it is not a substitute or an excuse for inaction. And nor is it a reason to delay what can be done today.

If we've learned anything from our recent times, it is that we don't know what tomorrow will bring. We need to build our lives with tomorrow in mind, *while doing justice to today*. The last thing that should happen is that we find ourselves at the end of our lives, having been patient throughout, and having achieved none of our goals or dreams. How do you know you will be alive tomorrow? How do you know you will be as healthy as you are today? How do you know you will have access to the resources you do today?

Are you still going to wait around for the perfect moment to present itself?

I want you to always keep in mind that time is *not* on your side. You have control only over this present moment, *now*. You cannot possibly know if you will have the next one. You have today, yes, and that could be it— there may or may not be a tomorrow.

Taking Control of Your Day

A "No Punches Pulled" approach to life absolutely requires that you control your days and, take your days head-on—with intention and purpose. You need to take charge of your day from the moment you wake up. Your morning routine matters more than you give it credit— your routines and habits will determine your success and happiness, not your wishes and dreams.

Make an honest assessment of how well you control your days using the following questions, so that you know where you've got to begin.

Q1 – Do you begin with the bigger picture?

Ask yourself, do you begin your day by noting down your thoughts and ideas on what you want to accomplish during the day? Or do you find yourself immediately lost in a plethora of emails or Instagram updates as soon as you've had your morning coffee? If you want to take control of your day, you naturally want to begin by planning out the bigger picture for the day ahead.

Q2 – Do you start the day with a smile?

If you're beginning each day on a tone of negativity, it's harder to stay in control as the day goes by. Protect your days, and especially your mornings, from anything that can put you off, whether it's a snarky email from a client or an irate remark from a colleague. Start your day on a note of gratitude—you'll see the difference in your energy through the day.

Q3 – Does your morning routine include exercise?

Getting your body moving and your heart pumping is an excellent way to start the day—it's proven to help you tackle the day with more energy and optimism.

Q4 – Do you give yourself daily reminders of what it would feel like to succeed?

Does your morning begin with affirmations? Are you constantly imagining what your success would look like? Can you see it clearly? You want to remind yourself daily what your success would feel like; it will do wonders to boost your determination to work toward your goals, no matter how bleak the day ahead looks.

Q5 – Do you prioritize strategizing over execution at the beginning of your day?

To make the most of each day, you need to plan as well as execute your tasks and goals. However, planning what you need to do at the beginning of the day when you're fully mindful and fresh makes for a better day of execution. Think before you do, and then do.

Q6 – Do you consciously protect boundaries from distractions and stress inducers as you go along your day?

In looking to stay on top of your day, how well are you able to keep aside harmful distractions? Build boundaries to keep out negative people and triggers—you can deal with these later, once you're done with what matters most in your day.

The NPP Toolbox: Build Control of Your Day

Remember, planning out your days and taking complete ownership of each day will help you be much more proactive, stay well rested and confident, strengthen your sense of purpose, and help you take ownership of your life.

It's time to get yourself equipped with proven action steps that will help you begin your day on a note of control, as well as teach you how to keep it in your control, no matter how unexpected the day turns out to be.

#1 – Schedule your day, on paper – make sure you spell it out

It's important to write down your goals for each day as you begin the day, because this brings you more advantages than you probably imagine. Spelling out your goals on paper makes you aware of the journey and your big purpose. Knowing what you want keeps you from spending the day in lethargy or on autopilot.

Putting pen to paper ensures you remember your goals, loud and clear, as the day goes by. When your goals are in front of you, they have a better chance of keeping you on track. So, write them down. Pin them up. Make them your screensaver. Build as many cues as you need to keep yourself on top of your day.

#2 – Plan out each day the night before

If you want to give yourself even more of a boost to kick off your day, plan out each day in advance. Spend a few minutes every night to plan the next day—and you've given yourself a head start before you've even woken up. To get the hang of this, begin by setting a reminder for each night, until this practice has become a habit.

#3 – Tackle your hardest task first

To give yourself a fighting chance to stay on top of all your days, even the hardest ones, begin each day by getting off your plate your hardest task for the day. You will feel more confident and less burdened as you continue your day.

#4 – Plan the day using the Pomodoro Technique or the Batching method

There are several productivity and time management techniques that can help you schedule your work. One such method is the Pomodoro Technique; it mentions that we should work in focused slots of twenty-five minutes, followed by five minutes of rest.

After you've implemented the Pomodoro cycle four times, give yourself a longer break. Take a fifteen-minute break or stop for lunch, and continue later with two to three more time blocks. With this strategy, you're in control of your day instead of external events pulling you away from the work that matters.

Another method is task batching, which is simply putting together tasks of a similar nature together, in one slot. You can write all your emails together at the end of the day, for instance, instead of checking and writing them several times throughout the day.

#5 – Carve out blocks of time for rest and fun

Every individual absolutely needs to take a breather and to reenergize the mind, in order to prevent burnout, no matter how ambitious or determined he or she is to win. Unwinding at regular intervals is not a luxury—it is a necessity. Remember the importance of this as you plan out each day.

#6 – Be realistic in your daily goals

While enthusiasm has its place, being overconfident or delusional about how much you can accomplish in one day will leave you feeling defeated at the end. So, try to be more realistic as you take on the day and remember that continuous progress that compounds is much more powerful in the long run than occasional or spontaneous bursts of passion.

#7 – Learn from your patterns of work

You want to observe what works best for you in your style of working. You don't have to do what everyone else is doing if it simply doesn't align with your pattern of working. You don't have to follow every strategy in this book. But you do have to figure out what techniques work best for your unique journey.

#8 – Work in sync with your natural productivity

For the best results, plan your work in sync with your natural cycle of productivity, and not against it. For instance, if you're a morning person, don't set up late-night meetings.

#9 – Plan and conduct your meetings smartly

Take a closer look at your calendar for the past few months and see how well your meetings are grouped. Do you have a recurring early morning meeting that stresses you out? Are you scheduling important meetings for late evenings when you're tired? Are you leading your meetings with clear agendas and ending with next steps and timelines articulated well?

#10 – Review and introspect regularly

Taking some time to quickly look back at how you're doing can be an excellent way to help you stay on top of your immediate future plans. If you can spend a few minutes every night on a daily review, great—or at least try to do it weekly.

Unless you reflect on what you're doing right or wrong, how can you make things better? It's alright if you failed to complete some tasks, or gave in too much to distractions, but think about how to fix this in the days to come.

Chapter takeaways

- You want to stop taking your bad days lightly and keep them from snowballing into larger chunks of time lost from your life.

- Taking charge of your day, when done repeatedly, helps you stay more proactive, keeps you well rested and confident, strengthens your sense of purpose, and helps you take ownership.

- Don't mistake patience for inaction, and don't let it serve as an excuse for procrastination. Patience is a virtue alongside deliberate, consistent action toward your goals.

- Plan your day out on the previous night. As you begin your day, write down your goals clearly. Experiment with various productivity and time management methods and choose which one works best in synchronization with your patterns of working.

- Tackle your most difficult tasks first, schedule your meetings efficiently, review how you're spending your days, and remember to set aside some time for fun.

Develop Your Obsession
(and do whatever it takes)

"If something is important enough, even if the odds are against you, you should still do it."

Elon Musk

Years ago, I awakened my obsession when I read Tony Robbins's amazing book *Awaken the Giant Within*. I discovered the book by accident; something told me to pick it up, and with the last twenty bucks I had, I walked out of that bookstore with a book that would change the course of my life.

Within weeks I was writing down my goals, practicing positive affirmations, and talking about success and the things that I was going to do. I turned my addiction for chaos into an addiction for learning. The more I discovered and implemented, the hungrier I became for knowledge and growth.

I would write out my goals over and over, refining my mission and purpose. The more I did this, the more I recognized patterns. My obsession was awakening and telling me what to do next. I felt like I had been a lost ship on the ocean in the middle of a storm and suddenly, there was light on land guiding me carefully toward safe shores.

Within weeks, I uncovered my deep-seated dream of wanting to travel the world, learn a new language, and write books that would help people achieve success. I was obsessed with my dream. I started planning my escape. I decided that one year from that day, I was getting on an airplane and leaving my safety net of work, relationships, friends, and family to pursue an obsession with living a great life.

At first, a lot of "what if" questions came to my mind. What if I ran out of money after I started traveling? What if I failed and had to start all over again? What if ...? I realized that these questions were the wrong questions to ask because they only built fear. I started to ask "how" and "what" questions instead. "How would I get to Thailand? What would I first do when I got there?"

I pinned up my vision board on my wall. I put up my goals, positivity quotes, and anything else I could find. I knew I had to start living the dream in my mind first before it became my reality.

To build your "No Punches Pulled" approach to life, you need to develop an obsession for your dreams—you need to awaken and commit to it. Make yourself obsessed with your success. Make yourself obsessed with becoming your best.

You can only be obsessed with something if you truly love it, whether it's a job, a target net worth number, a painting, a degree, a fitness goal, or a relationship. Only if you truly care about something will you persist against the odds. Remember—it should be *you* that's obsessed with your goal, and not someone else influencing you.

With such obsession, *success is certain*.

Learning from the heroes

Think of the most successful people in the world. I promise you none of them got where there wanted to be without being obsessed with their dreams, visions and goals. It's said that Muhammed Ali used to repeat "I'm the best, I'm the best" because he wanted to believe it himself first, so that he could go out and beat the best. If you truly want to be all in and will stop at nothing, you need to light that fire within you that will help you crush everything that gets in your way.

"You must become your own champion and cheerleader before anyone else starts cheering you on."

Michael Jordan is the best basketball player on the planet because he became obsessed with becoming the best and let nothing get in his way. Elon Musk is making history by building the future because he became obsessed with creating the future, and no matter how many failures he endured, he continued to push the boundaries of space and science.

Best-selling author and world-class speaker **Mel Robbins**, in her book *The High Five Habit*, says that "the #1 reason people fail to reach their goals is that they don't believe they are worthy of having them. They are not obsessed enough to make it happen."

Make a list of the famous people you know; there are hundreds and thousands of them. From classical composers Mozart and Bach to modern sports figures such as Babe Ruth and Muhammad Ali, actors and movie directors, Steve Jobs and Serena Williams, Bill Gates, Jim

Henson, Steven Spielberg, John Williams, Stephen King, J. K. Rowling, Wayne Gretzky, and Mark Zuckerberg. Obsession had all of them. They wouldn't be where they are today, if it were not for that obsession to go beyond where everyone else stopped pushing the boundary. That is what obsession does to you.

Using your obsession to become a master

Your obsession aligns with and fuels your purpose—the reason you were born. Stephen King is one of the greatest writers of our time. He has written over 70 books and sold over 450 million copies. But he wouldn't have succeeded at just about anything; it was his purpose in life to be a great writer. Serena Williams is one of the greatest tennis players who ever lived, but it is tennis she mastered. Not golf or bowling nor tennis.

Take any super-achiever and look at what they have mastered. You will see a singular driving purpose and an all-consuming obsession behind their success. You will see raw grit: a potent combination of **passion, determination**, and **perseverance**.

No such thing as an overnight success

In a culture wrapped tightly around social media, people get carried away by "overnight sensations." They look at winners in amazement and chalk up their success to a born talent or an unfair competitive advantage. They'll say some just got lucky.

While it's certainly true that these people got lucky breaks, it's also true that they set up everything to make luck happen. They were fully prepared when their opportunities presented themselves; they had trained for it for years, if not for decades.

The difference between obsession and motivation

Obsession and motivation are similar, but not the same. Motivation rides entirely on emotion; it's there one minute and gone the next. It's unreliable. Obsession, on the other hand, is closer to hyper-focus. You live, breathe, and act according to the very thing you are obsessed about.

Obsession is that burning drive deep down in your gut that, if you listen closely, sounds like someone screaming inside of you. Turning off your obsession by blocking it out with distractions or addictions won't work. Ignoring your obsession to succeed will build up into a quiet desperation, but turning it into the wave of your greatest passion will make you **unbreakable**.

So, while waiting to be motivated is like waiting for the tide to come in before you set your boat to sail, obsession makes you *drag your boat out to meet the water.*

Another big difference between motivation and obsession is that when you're obsessed, you're willing to pay whatever price it takes to make it. The name of the game is called "whatever it takes." You will do anything to top the charts, beat the competition, and push the naysayers aside when they tell you to slow down.

It doesn't matter if you're not obsessed with your dreams yet—you're beginning to understand what obsession is, you've felt it within you a few times, you know exactly what it feels like to have something awaken inside of you and fill you with excitement. Maybe your obsession feels unnatural to you. Maybe it doesn't feel real. But it is real, and it won't go away—it will wait for you to uncover it.

Real obsession for success, the kind that turns Da Vinci or Pablo into world-class artists, or Charlie Chaplin into a world-class entertainer, doesn't just go away. You can ignore it, but once awakened, it reminds you it's there.

Always remember that only *you* are responsible for your success. Nobody is going to save you. Nobody is going to show you how to succeed. Nobody is going to believe in your dreams if you don't. They may support you. They may encourage you. They may correct you. But they aren't responsible for you. You owe it to yourself to be obsessed with your dream and to chase, build and win your best life.

You don't have to "discover" your obsession. You just need to awaken it.

You need to know that obsession lives in you, lives in me, and within the thousands out there who are still confused. Many will ignore their obsessions long enough and will burn out that flame. But few will be lucky enough to fully awaken to their obsession, and this is going to include you.

How will you know when you've tapped into your obsession? That's easy. It's all you think about. It consumes your thoughts. You are working on your obsession mentally, even when doing other work for someone else. Obsession is your awakening. It is when your mind is fully fixated on your mission. You know exactly what needs to be done without writing it down or carrying reminders. Your gift of obsession is what makes your inner "beast" come alive.

You need to get obsessed, *now*, with destroying your life on average. You need to get obsessed with shaping your life the way it is meant to be. You aren't going to live your dream life and find happiness by buying more stuff, earning credit at the bank, or taking a dream vacation you have to spend six months working for just to pay off. You're only going to build your dream life by living your purpose, fueled by your obsession, whatever it may take.

You're going to learn how your obsession will help you and how you can fully activate it. It's time to awaken to your fullest potential.

The Power of Obsession

Why does it help to be obsessed with what you want? Here are 8 reasons to develop an obsession toward your best goals.

1. Obsession helps you grow faster

When you think of and work toward one and only one thing, even if you make a ton of mistakes along the way, you'll grow faster, and thus increase your likelihood of success.

2. Obsession drives creativity

When you're obsessed, second best simply isn't good enough. You're insatiable.

You won't accept something until you think it is perfect. Think of Steve Jobs. Think of Elon Musk. Think of Lady

Gaga. When you want something badly enough, you'll unleash your creative best.

Obsession gets you to chart your own course. You aren't bothered with what others are doing. You won't be afraid to reject the way things have always been done by the majority.

3. Obsession helps you believe that what you want is going to happen

The more deeply you believe something to be true, the more likely it is to unfold in your reality.

4. Obsession makes you brave

Something wonderful happens with obsession; you stop overthinking and you stop being afraid. You feel more courageous than you ever have before, and it is precisely this bravery that opens doors and takes you places.

5. Obsession makes you more productive

When you're obsessed with something, you're likely to become the most efficient you've ever been, because you want to achieve your goal, no matter what. Your desire fuels all other aspects of your life and makes you operate at your productive best.

6. Obsession helps you focus

A laser-like obsession is a secret of the most successful people on earth. There's no room for distractions—even with regard to different areas where your input is needed for work. You're focused on one thing at a time. Obsession makes it easier to say "no" to things that are not aligned with your goal. And that naturally makes you more successful.

7. Obsession makes you responsible

When you're obsessed with something, you're not going to spend time making excuses, blaming others, or dillydallying. You're going to take complete ownership of whatever you want to achieve. You'll find ways to get through your hurdles, whether that requires reshuffling your team, going back to school, or seeking out the right mentors.

You want to become the best you can, as quickly as you can. You've got no time to waste with ifs and buts. Obsessive people are obsessive learners; they never stop experimenting and improving their skills and tactics. They take complete responsibility.

8. Obsession gives you a competitive advantage

Say you're up against more talented competitors. You'll still beat them if you outwork them, and to outwork them, you need to be obsessed with what you're doing. Most people give up as soon as things start to get tough. The obsessed don't. They are the few who make it through while others fall by the wayside.

It always helps to remember that all of us are created equal—it is our efforts, passions, habits, discipline, and choices that differentiate us, and all of these can be fueled by obsession.

Your NPP Obsession Building Kit

Now that you know what it means to be obsessed and why it's important in chasing your dreams, it's time to learn exactly how to build the obsession to become great. You'll find several action prompts below that will help you activate your obsession. You can become a master at one or learn to excel at a handful of them.

1. Decide that what you want is possible, no matter what it may be

No matter how impossible something may seem to you at the outset, your passion will make it probable, and then possible. When Elon Musk said, "We're going to Mars" or when Walter Disney envisioned a happy world, it seemed impossible. They then fought all odds to make their vision a reality.

2. Set big goals – you'll figure out how to get to them

If you were to reverse engineer your future, what would it look like today? What is the biggest goal? Ask yourself if you could have anything, what would it be? What have you always wanted? Write down your goals. The bigger and scarier, the better. It just means you'll level up to reach them.

3. Give yourself permission to chase your dream

You should need no validation or permission to chase any of your dreams—they are yours and yours alone to believe in and bring to life. But if you still need permission to begin, I'm giving it to you right now. You have no time to lose. You don't know what will happen next week. You need to begin chasing your dream today—you've waited around to see what happens long enough.

4. Relentlessly chase one goal at a time – be prepared for resistance

The time for hedging is over—it's time to commit to a single course of action with all you've got. Your chance to succeed increases with your level of commitment because it parallels an increase in effort and knowledge. If you have a clear goal, you'll build a clear strategy. Calculated risk is not harmful, recklessness is.

5. Focus on what you want every single day

Visualize your goals. Focus is power, and it is the difference between hitting your mark and coming close to it. Do you want to "almost succeed," or do you want to "hit your mark" head-on? Focus channels your thoughts and energies to make it happen.

6. Use journaling to build clarity

Start keeping a journal and write down your goals, not just once but every day. Repeat your goals to yourself and write them down so many times that they become a part of you. You'll be better able to identify what you really want because it's in front of you and not in your head.

Only a small handful of people reach this level of clarity, passion, and commitment. Maybe 1% of the 1% write down their goals every day. It doesn't matter what you start writing—tap your inner power and remember a time when you wanted something so bad it set you on fire. That fire is still there. You think it's gone but it's not. You can reignite it.

7. Build a system of feedback loops

An important part of developing an obsession with something is to get into the practice of maintaining a feedback loop, whereby you're continuously thinking of how you can improve at something. The world is changing faster than ever before; it's easy to get carried away with a little success, not knowing that the wheel is about to turn. It's important to constantly question any internal biases and reach out to get real feedback.

8. Get rid of fear

Fear and obsession don't go hand in hand—one drives out the other. A small amount of fear is healthy—it shows you that what you're chasing matters to you, and keeps you taking a sensible course of action. Fear encourages you to plan better and to manage risk better. In small doses, it's good for you. But if it's crippling you, you need to address it, now.

9. Leverage the power of compounding

Lastly, remember that extraordinary people are not made in the blink of an eye. It's years and even decades of work that goes in and compounds, along with an obsession to never quit. No matter how ordinary you think you are, getting better by just 1% every day across the aspects of your life you care about the most, whether it's your fitness, emotional health, finances, or creative satisfaction, can take you miles ahead when cumulated. Always remember and leverage the power of compounding.

Everyone's obsession is different. Some people are aware of their obsessions and commit to them, whereas others' obsessions are crowded out by the noise. Listen to what

you truly want, and go after it, "No Punches Pulled."
You now know how to wake up the beast within.

Chapter takeaways

- You don't need to find or discover your obsession—it
  already exists within you and has been reaching out to
  you. You only need to awaken it.

- Obsession and motivation are different. Motivation
  relies on emotion and is volatile. Obsession is all-
  consuming, makes you unbreakable and unstoppable,
  and gets you to your goals, no matter what it takes to
  make it.

- Your obsession aligns with and fuels your purpose; it
  drives you to become a master.

- You want to develop an obsession when it comes to
  chasing your goals because it helps you grow faster,
  makes you more creative, makes you more
  responsible, productive, focused, brave, and gives you
  an edge over your competition.

- Use as many tools from your NPP obsession building
  kit as you can. Begin by deciding that anything you
  want is possible. Write it down. Chase each goal
  relentlessly, one at a time. Practice journaling. Get
  feedback. Get rid of fear. And remember the magic
  of compounding.

The "NPP" Conclusion

A Quick Recap: Your "No Punches Pulled" guide to life

I want to end this book by walking you through the key lessons of the "No Punches Pulled" approach to living a life that is uncommon, thriving, boundless, and abundant. It doesn't matter where you're beginning— whether you're at ground zero or well on your way to your goals.

Internalize as many concepts as you can from this book and begin to live them to see outstanding results and changes in yourself, your mind, and your growth. Here's a summary to arm you with all you need to know.

Building clarity is the first step to success. To get you what you want, no matter what it is, you need to first know exactly what you desire, and you need to commit to pursuing it. You also need to be willing to pay the price to achieve this goal.

Most people will get through life without figuring out exactly what they want, and even the ones who do will lose out because they will want to win their prize without fighting the fight. Decide to build clarity—this means sitting with your thoughts and designing a clear picture for your future.

For those entirely committed to their dream, there's no room for, and no need for, a plan B—so **throw away**

your plan B. This will ensure you're giving your all to plan A, not making half-hearted attempts, not giving yourself permission to quit, listening to your heart, and channelizing your time, energy, resources, and creativity in one focused direction.

Everything that occurs in the world around you first comes to life in your mind. This is why you must **go to war with your mind**, each morning, and control your thoughts, instead of letting them control you. Learn how to let thoughts and emotions pass by, without needing to react to each one. Learn how to stop giving in to each distraction or trigger. To succeed, you need to build a bulletproof mind, one that functions as an ally, and not your enemy.

The standards you set for yourself will set the course for your future. You will only become what you know you are worth becoming, and you will only have what you believe you deserve to have. So, **set the highest standards possible** for yourself, now, in the present— and trust yourself to grow into them.

For the highest level of success, practice isn't enough— you need to **commit to deliberate practice**, even on, and especially on, your worst days. It doesn't matter if someone else has more advantages or resources than you—if you decide to outwork them, no matter what, you've won half the battle. Deliberate practice can be your biggest competitive advantage because very few people have what it really takes to commit to their goals to the exclusion of all else.

We all have a dark side within us, and suppressing it is harmful. On the contrary, you want to **embrace your**

dark side because it can teach you valuable lessons and bring important insights to life about your hopes and dreams that might have, for various reasons, been overlooked. Acknowledge and learn from your dark side, but feed the light.

Your life depends on the choices you make at **crucial turning points**; it is these decisions that set the course of your life. Opportunity abounds, and nothing is ever "the end"—but the same moment, and the exact same choice or circumstance will not occur again. Train your mind to embrace challenges instead of running from them, seize each day knowing it will never return, and learn to build confidence, clarity, and calmness so that you make decisions to live your best life.

If you want what everyone around you does not have, you have to be willing to do what everyone around you does not do. Get ready to train to win. Get ready to **outwork everyone else**. Know that there's no room for excuses in the 1% club.

The most successful people on the planet got where they are by awakening the beast within them, by **developing their obsessions to become the best**. They did whatever it took to master their craft, stopped viewing success as an overnight feat, and committed to putting in the work. They used their obsession to grow faster, be more creative, brave, productive, focused and responsible than their peers.

Stop taking your time for granted. You need to **stick to your optimal schedule with hyper-focus**, and you need to build momentum to have an edge. Setting plans and goals doesn't matter unless you take aligned action.

To seize each day, learn how to **control the day** with deliberation, confidence, and urgency. Realize that patience is not an excuse for inaction or procrastination, but must be combined with deliberate action, day after day.

There can be no success without growth, and no growth without discomfort, so begin pushing yourself to get familiar with, and even to **thrive within, discomfort**. We tend to stay within the realm of what we know and understand, but our comfort zone is not where growth occurs. An avoidance of discomfort, change, or new situations generally stems from fear, so you need to understand and address your fears.

A Call to Action

Now that we've recapped the key concepts covered in the book, I want to remind you that absolutely nothing will change *unless you take action*.

Making the best plans and refining them until they're perfect won't help. Thinking about the best sequence to follow your strategies in won't help. Beginning to passionately execute the strategies as best as you can, starting *now*, is what will make all the difference.

Build Clarity and Discover The Power of Laser-Focused Attention

Figure out your "why"—without this, you have no motivation to fuel you. Write down what you envision, and make your goals as specific as you can, so that you can take and measure aligned action.

Throw Away Plan B, and Go All In and Take the Island

First, think carefully about plan A. Spend as much time as you need, but once you have it figured out, commit to it exclusively and entirely. Let your fear of not having a backup motivate you. Get better at managing risks, and go out there and build a support system you can rely on as you begin to chase your one true dream.

Go to War with Your Mind Every Morning

Don't run from difficult questions and situations—be honest with yourself. Realize what thoughts are holding you back and why. Ensure that whatever you're chasing aligns with the values you truly believe in, and that you aren't setting goals for others' sakes. Feed your mind well, and exercise every morning or as often as you can to keep yourself and your mind alert.

Accelerate Your Standards by 1000%

Only you get to decide what you deserve—so decide, now. Stop allowing yourself to settle. Accept that you will pay a very high price by lying to yourself, and not living up to the standards you know you are capable of reaching and want to live by.

Implement the Habit of Deliberate Practice, and Know your Success is an Inside Job

Get rid of any mental barriers you may have of a "breaking point." Focus on improving by 1% every single day, ask for help when you're stuck, make it as easy as you can to commit to your practice, and remember that your well-being is top priority.

Understand Your Dark Side and Feed the Right Wolf

Listen to what you find in your anger, envy, hatred, and sadness. Decide that you are not a victim. Decide to view everything from a positive and uplifting perspective. And keep reminding yourself that no matter what happens around you, the world within you is entirely in your control.

Cross Over the Point of No Return; Make Pivotal Decisions Well

Practice being uncomfortable—don't expect yourself to suddenly be able to make big decisions with ease, but rather, build your appetite for risk and more informed decision-making by cultivating habits such as meditation and journaling.

Train to Win and to Outwork Everyone Else

Learn how to completely rethink failure—there's no room for fear of failure in your journey. To get to the top 1%, begin by defining your own version of success. Then, take ownership, let go of things outside your control while capitalizing on those within, ask for feedback, use competition correctly, and focus on long-term plays and not instant gratification traps.

Develop Your Obsession to Become the Best

No matter what anyone else says, promise yourself that what you want is possible. Give yourself permission—know that you deserve your wildest dreams, and believe they will come true, because you will make them. Be prepared for resistance, but chase one goal at a time relentlessly, with clarity, every day, knowing that your efforts will compound.

Hyper-focus and Live by Your Optimal Schedule to Build Momentum

Focus on one thought—one goal—and how achieving it makes you feel, for 17 seconds; practice unwavering focus on this goal so that you reinforce it within your mind. Plan out your days in 15-minute slots to make the most of them, review what you have been working on and how efficiently you've been spending your time, stick to the most important tasks instead of taking on too much and overwhelming yourself, and prioritize your work around importance and urgency, while getting rid of the nonessential.

Take Control of Your Day and Build Intention into Your Purpose

Begin your day with the big picture in mind, and with a smile. Remember what it would feel like to succeed, and give yourself your best chance of making the most of each day by cutting out the distractions, whether physical or digital.

Plan out your days in advance, tackle the hardest tasks first, use time management tools that work best for you, work in sync with your natural productivity patterns, and remember to rest and have fun.

Train Your Mind to Get Comfortable with Becoming Uncomfortable

In undertaking your NPP discomfort challenge, your first stage is acceptance; you want to learn to put yourself in uncomfortable situations, step by step. Do this with one more rep, one more page of reading, one more meeting—do it slowly, but steadily. Embrace your thoughts and fears. Get your finances and other essentials in order, and get organized.

Once you've prepped your mind and stretched it a bit to be comfortable with being uncomfortable, it's time to hit the gas. Go looking for challenges. Let your efforts snowball. Do what you've never done. Celebrate your progress and keep improving with repetition.

Lastly, smile through your journey, even in the darkest times; realize how well you're building yourself and how powerful you are becoming.

I hope this book has encouraged you to grow in your journey with much more determination and grit, and helped you ground yourself for extraordinary success with advice culled from philosophy, science, and decades of practical experience.

I wish you well on your awakening to your boundless potential—you are ready, for the best of who you are becoming is yet to come.

Scott Allan

"Champions aren't made in the gyms. Champions are made from something they have deep inside them—a desire, a dream, a vision. They have to have the skill, and the will. But the will must be stronger than the skill."

—**Muhammad Ali**

Also by Scott Allan

Available wherever books, eBooks and audiobooks are sold.

Conquer Imposter Syndrome, Develop a Resilient
Mindset, and Fail Forward With Confidence

Available wherever books, eBooks and audiobooks are sold.

Develop an Unbeatable Mindset, Transcend Difficult Obstacles, and Defeat Your Resistance to Change

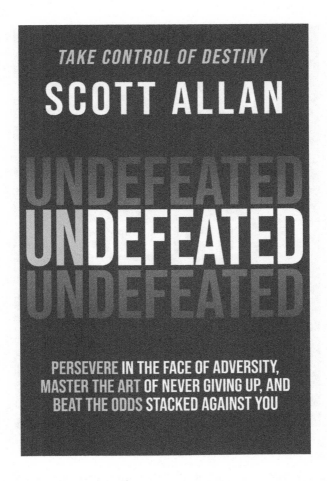

Available wherever books, eBooks and audiobooks are sold.

Break the Procrastination Habit, Accelerate Your Productivity, and Take Control of Your Life NOW.

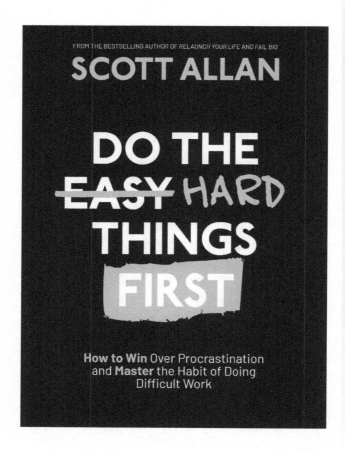

Available wherever books, eBooks and audiobooks are sold.

About Scott Allan

Scott Allan is a bestselling author who has a passion for teaching, building life skills, and inspiring others to take charge of their lives.

Scott's mission is to give people the strategies needed to design the life they want through choice.

He believes successful living is a series of small, consistent actions taken every day to build a thriving lifestyle with intentional purpose.

By taking the necessary steps and eliminating unwanted distractions that keep you stuck, you are free to focus on the essentials.

You can connect with Scott online:

Email: ScottAllan@scottallaninternational.com

Instagram

https://www.instagram.com/scottallanauthor/

Facebook

https://www.facebook.com/scottallanauthor

ScottAllan SA

Made in the USA
Las Vegas, NV
10 January 2022

40983623R00104